LIVING WITH GHOSTS

PREFACE

As far back as I can remember, it was a scary place to live.

Even as a young child, there was something about our house that just wasn't right.

In the daytime, it was bearable.

With family around, and sunshine beaming through the windows, it helped to lighten the mood.

But it didn't stop the feeling that you were being watched.

It didn't stop the feeling that there was someone or something that was in the house, that didn't belong.

Even visitors felt uneasy. An overwhelming feeling of permeation filled every room. And it went deep.

We were told that many years ago, before the house was built, the ground upon which it stands was once a cemetery. It speaks for itself. But it wasn't just the house that was possessed.

This book will give you an insight into some of what my family had to encounter, living with the other side.

M.

It was the school summer holidays.

As expected, the weather was perfect. The sun was shining, with the slightest hint of a breeze. And back in 70's England, there wasn't such a thing as humidity.

Children and adults alike could exert themselves in all aspects of work and play, and the heat of the day was never a factor.

But for me, being the only daughter, with three older brothers to contend with, and an over-possessive Father, I would only be allowed to venture out as far as the back garden.
This was my boundary.
Whether my Father was home or not, I would not have dared to defy his authority.
So while my brothers were playing at the park, or round their friend's houses, I had to be content with playing with my dolls in my bedroom, or in the back garden, catching butterflies, or sitting on the doorstep reading.

It was great when I had friends round.
We would invent all sorts of games to keep ourselves amused.
But that didn't happen often, as most of them wanted to be out in the street with the other kids.
So I valued the friends that chose to spend their time with me.

This particular afternoon, everyone was home, including Dad.

It had been a terrible time for him, as he had just lost one of his sister's, who had died suddenly, and painfully.
He was particularly close to this sister, who we will call Aunty Louise.
He came from a big family of 6 daughters, and two sons.

Aunty Louise was a lovely lady, and I remember her well.
She was kind, and loving, and often stayed at our house.
She was a timid lady, and easily upset.
But would always be there for anyone that needed her help.
I shall never forget her.

Unfortunately, her battle for life was lost, at the young age of 49.

We knew the day had come, because at 7am that Sunday morning, the exact time she died, our dog started howling, and did not stop for about an hour. And as I grew up, I realised that one of the old housewife tales was, if a dog howled like that for no reason, it meant someone in the family had died.

Our dog had felt it ...

Although I was very young, I had grown close to my Aunty, and I missed her terribly. So I couldn't possibly imagine what my Father was going through.
But he was struggling.
And it hurt to see him this way.

We were watching television in the front room.
The day was warm, and the slight breeze through the windows was just enough to keep us cool.

Suddenly, without reason, the door that lead to the stairs threw itself open, and slammed against the wall.

We all jumped and turned around.
We looked at each other in disbelief.

There was no wind at all.

My Father told my brother (We will call him Colin), to close the door again.

He did so, and we all turned around, and tried to forget what had just happened, and continued to watch the television.

Once again, the door flew open, and slammed against the wall.
It was done with such anger, even my Father could not have done it that hard.

At this point, the television was turned off.
He told us to go and sit with Mum in the corner of the room, the opposite side to where the door was.

He took hold of the armchair, and started to drag it across the room. He was a very strong man, and even he was struggling to move it.

At this point, I think we all knew what he was about to do.

He finally jammed the armchair against the door, and walked back to the other side of the room where we were huddled around Mum.

What happened next, still to this very day, haunts me.

Dad spoke in a loud voice, and called to his dead Father to move the chair.

Nothing happened.

He called to another family member who had passed away, to move the chair.

Nothing happened.

Then he called to his sister, my Aunty Louise, who had passed away, to move the chair.

The chair ended up in the middle of the room, and the door slammed against the wall...

I will never forget that moment as long as I live.

I believe, for me, that was my first real encounter with the other side.

And as a small child, this was a very hard thing to come to terms with.

I already understood death. And that was scary enough for me.

But to think that people who had died, and were laid to rest in the ground, could actually come back and do these things, was beyond my understanding.

Everyone was in shock.

After my initial scream, I just remember looking at Mum and Dad, from one to the other, waiting for an explanation that wasn't to come.

I remember Dad saying that his sister wasn't resting. And he believed it was because of what happened to her while she was alive.

Thinking about it now, and the horrific things that happened to her, and the young age she was suddenly taken, it is no wonder that my Aunty was not at rest.

She was snatched from life in her prime.

Her spirit was still crying out for unspoken words, and uneaten bread.

"Between Worlds" is how I see it.

This was to be the first of many times that I would feel my Aunty with me.

And still do …..

This pre-war house was creepy enough as it was, let alone to think that we had invisible visitors along for the ride.

And now my whole family had witnessed *the armchair event*, we just didn't know what to expect next. But we expected something. We knew it wasn't going to stop there.

The door to the other side had opened, for whatever reason.
And the supernatural from the unknown world was flooding through every room.

It was really scaring me. So much, I had become too frightened to go to bed.

I had my own room. My three brothers had each other! They all shared a room. So when bedtime came, I would lie there for ages, trying to sleep.
But a child's mind is very active with imagination,

and I would imagine all sorts of scenarios happening should I fall to sleep.

It was ok while I could hear Mum and Dad still talking downstairs. If I could just go to sleep before they came to bed. That was great.

But it didn't always work. And that moment, when I would hear them climbing the stairs to retire for the night, would send shivers down my whole body.

I would feel sick with fear. Oh God, I am going to be the only one awake again!

After the click of the light switch, I knew there would be silence.

The switch was my signal to make my move.

I would go into their room, and tell Dad I was scared.

Not once did he ever question it, or make me go back to my bed.

He would let me get in-between him and Mum.
And that was it!

The fear would melt away immediately, and I would snuggle up between them, and sleep like a baby.

No more fears. With my parents around me, I was safe.

Till the next time …..

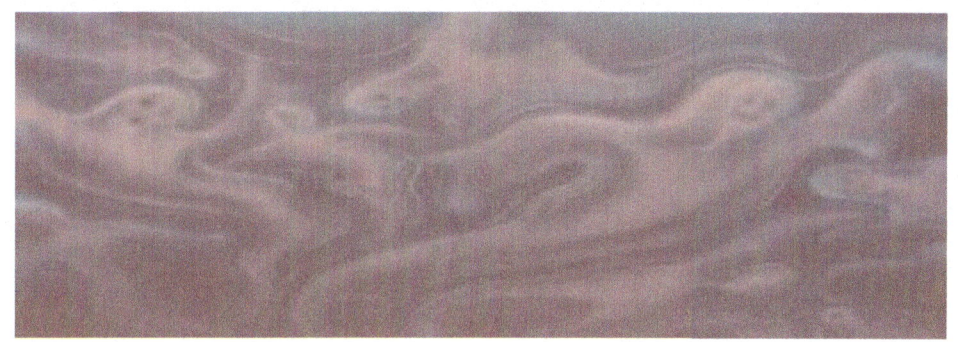

It was a cold afternoon.

Mum had the open fire burning, and the front room was warm and cozy.

She had laid a blanket on top of the rug by the fire, and was teaching us how to play the game of Ludo.

Dad was at work. So it was Mum, me, and my brothers all enjoying an afternoon together.

During the day, with everyone there, that room was lovely.

Mum was the decorator, and always made sure the house looked nice.

We didn't have much money, but what we did have, my parents made sure we were clothed, fed and happy. And the house was spotless.

I loved being at home with everyone. We were a close family, and it meant everything to us.

There was only one thing that made me feel uneasy about that room.

We had a big picture above the fireplace, of Jesus Christ.

It was a beautiful picture.

But the eyes would haunt you.

During the day, the eyes were fixed. They just looked forward, as the painting portrayed.

But during the night, it was a different story.

It didn't matter where you were in that room, those eyes would follow you.

It truly felt like the picture had come alive.

It was very unnerving to say the least.

Back then, I remember thinking that it was a ghost of the house, and they were using the picture to see us through.

However, my parents loved the picture and it stayed above the fireplace.

So this particular afternoon, because we were in the front room, I purposely avoided looking at the picture.

I always did.

We were enjoying ourselves immensely, playing the game with Mum.

When all of a sudden, there was a big smashing sound above us, as something was hurled against the fireplace wall, and shattered into a thousand pieces on the floor around us.

We all jumped up, wondering whatever had happened.

Mum made sure none of us were hurt, and we weren't. Luckily.

There was no one else in the house.

The only door that was open was the one that led to the kitchen.

The back door was still locked, and there was no one there.

Mum busied herself clearing up all the glass, while we sat looking at one another in total shock.

I remember Mum saying afterwards that it was an ash tray that had been thrown against the wall.

Whoever threw it must have been very angry, because that was thrown with some force.

Why would anyone want to hurt us? Was it meant to hurt us, or get our attention?

But we weren't hurt at all, not by the falling glass. If it had been thrown lower, it would have hit one of us direct, that's for sure.

Our *visitor* was having a bad day. And I guess they wanted us to know.

And we couldn't help, as we knew nothing of the problem!

Maybe that was what's known as a *Poltergeist*.

In folklore and paranormal studies, a poltergeist phenomenon alludes to the
apparent yet unexplained manifestation of multiple force reactions caused by a seemingly invisible entity. Most accounts of poltergeist manifestations involve such force being triggered at objects, usually household (destruction and relocation of furniture, levitation of cutlery, knocking on the doors), although some seem to describe accompanying hallucinations, as well as physical attacks on human witnesses.
Such actions can include pinching, biting, hitting and tripping the victim, or producing sentient noises (moaning, laughing, talking etc.) without clear source.

 Poltergeists occupy numerous niches in cultural folklore, and have traditionally been described as troublesome spirits who, unlike ghosts, haunt a particular person instead of a specific location.
Such alleged poltergeist manifestations have been reported in many cultures and countries including the United States, Japan, Brazil, Australia, and most European nations.
The earliest recorded cases date back to the 1st century.

Well, it certainly seemed like we had ourselves a Poltergeist!

But we couldn't for a second, think that my Aunty would be doing such things to us.

She wouldn't. And that was that.

She loved us. She was close to us. She was timid and shy, and certainly wouldn't dream of hurling heavy glass at us, no matter how bad she was feeling.

So as far as we were concerned, we had gained ourselves yet another entity in the house of fear.

Could it be that the cemetery the house was built upon had come alive?

Were they angry with us for living there? To our knowledge, there was only one other family that had lived in that house before us, but we didn't get a chance to meet them, or ask them if they had experienced anything like this. Or even why they moved ….

We lived in that house for over twenty years, and not once did any neighbour complain of such events. And everyone knew everyone in that street.

So either we were the only unfortunate ones. Or people weren't talking ….

It was beginning to get very worrying, if this was what we had to look forward to!

The room that my brothers slept in was the biggest bedroom.

My eldest brother slept in a single bed opposite the door.

The other two slept in a double bed across the room by the window.

On the opposite wall to the double bed, stood a white wardrobe.

This wardrobe was huge, and practically went from ceiling to floor.

I remember stencils of cartoon characters on the front of the doors.

But one of the doors had a tendency to fall open of its own accord.

Nothing spooky!

Just that the wardrobe was getting old, and was well used.

One night, my brother (We will call him Phillip), woke up during the night, and for no apparent reason, was wide awake.

His eyes fell on the wardrobe in front of him.
One of the doors was half open as usual.

But something was different.

There was someone/something standing inside it …..

Phillip rubbed his eyes, thinking that he was dreaming, and looked again.

It was still there, in all its glory.

Phillip was petrified and didn't dare move.
The only thing he could think of, was to wake Colin up, who he thought was asleep next to him.

Phillip, as quietly as he could, gently nudged Colin's arm, whispering "Colin ... Colin"

Only to be met with the reply from Colin -
"I know, I've seen it too" …..

They both pulled the covers half way up their faces and just laid there frozen on the spot for what seemed like forever.

This ghost-like apparition was transparent.
So there wasn't a clear view of the face.

But they believed the figure was that of a woman.

No words were spoken.
So we never knew why she appeared to my brothers that night.

It has been said many times before, that when some people pass over, they find it hard to communicate with the living, and have to learn this process.

This can take a while.
And during this time, they will learn how to poke and prod us, move objects around, and scare the daylights out of us, without being able to actually tell us who they are, or what they want.

They can appear as transparent, when they first walk among us, appearing as solid matter once they find their way around the dimension they move in.

As written by Constantly Working with Spirit, they are capable of anything.

They will come to you as they wish you to see them. So they can be any age they wish to be.

In a solid matter, they can touch you, talk to you, and listen to you.

Even deceased pets visit us as we would remember them when they were with us on earth.

Some spirits come to us as orbs of light, and can be different colours.

They can move things when they are in solid matter, or just as an energy….

Whatever the case or circumstance, they find their way through, and eventually some of us earthlings experience their presence.

The frightening thing for us is that it almost always seems to be the case that they do this during the night.

Most of us wouldn't be at all frightened if it were always to happen through the day.

But for the world of spirit, our most vulnerable time is when we are relaxed and more receptive and able to be approached.
And this comes with sleep and tiredness.

If they cannot reach us while we are awake, they will reach us in our dreams…

One evening, a friend of Dad's had come round.
Let's call him John.

There wasn't much that scared this man. He had slept on gravestones when he first lost his Mum. He had worked in a morgue in London, where he had to stay overnight, taking care of dead bodies, and making sure no one got into the building, and stole the elaborate jewels that were draped on the bodies.

There really wasn't much that could phase John in the slightest.

Until now ….

He had just lost his Dad. He had been dead for two days.

John had gone round to his Dad's house, to sort out his belongings.

But when he got there, the moment he walked in, the light blew in the bedroom.

Then the light went bang in the bathroom.

He felt his Dad all around him, like he was standing there with him.

He tried to ignore it, and began to gather together some of his things, and bag them up.

It was getting dark, so he walked over to pull the curtains together.

But as he was about to reach them, they suddenly drew themselves together.
And that was all that John could take.

He ran out of that house, and never went back.

He came straight to our house, and told us what had happened.

He was really shook up, and Mum made him sit down, and gave him a cup of tea.

We had never seen John like this. He was physically shaken from his experience.

So Mum and Dad sat with him and tried to calm him down.

Dad had kicked off his shoes in front of him, and was sat on the sofa.

None of us were prepared for what was about to happen.

Dad's shoes were sat between us, and the television, exactly where he had kicked them off before he had sat down.

All of a sudden, while they were talking to John, my Dad's shoes, both of them, suddenly raised themselves off of the floor about a foot into the air, and dropped to the ground again.

The first thing my Mum said was "God John, you've brought your Dad with you".

Poor John was freaked out all over again. And for the first time, I even see fear on my Dad's face, and that was not good!

Everyone just sat there looking at this pair of shoes, expecting them to move again.

They didn't.

But they didn't need to. The damage had been done.

Another strange phenomenon had hit our lives, and there was no explanation whatsoever.

Other than the obvious that is ……

This is where we found out that our *visitors* could follow us outside of the house too…

Every few weeks, at the weekend, we would travel to London to visit relatives.

Although I loved the fact that we were going to see family, I absolutely detested travelling, and more than likely felt sick through most of the journey there.

Once we arrived, I was absolutely fine, and enjoyed the day. And as it was usually late evening by the time we made our way home, I travelled much better at this hour of the night.
And a lot of the time, I would fall asleep anyway.

Well this was one of those typical days.

We had had a fantastic time in London, shopping, and visiting family till it was time to come home.

It was around midnight as we left London and headed home.

It was cold weather, and the early morning air was bringing in a mist across the windscreen.

By the time we got to the M1 motorway, the fog had come down so fast and so thick, we couldn't see more than 3 feet in front of the car.

This was a new experience. We had never had to drive home in weather conditions like this. It was treacherous. But we had to get home.

Back then, thankfully, there wasn't the amount of cars on the road that there are today.

But Dad still had to be very cautious, as he was so restricted to what he could see. He must have been driving the slowest he had ever driven in his life.

We would have been going faster if we were walking …

Mum was up front, trying her best to be another set of eyes for Dad.

We were huddled in the back under blankets, comfortably lying on each other, but aware of what was going on ahead.

Suddenly, Dad seemed to speed up.

As we all looked out of the window, we see that the weather had not changed, and the fog was still treacherously surrounding us within 3 feet of the car.

Mum suddenly sat up in alarm, as Dad seemed to be driving faster and faster.

We couldn't see a thing! So how could he!

Mum had seen enough, and told Dad to slow down, because he had the children in the car.

Dad's reply sent us cold …

"It's not me driving the car"

"What are you talking about"! came the reply from my Mum's obvious and expected fearful voice.

"It's not me driving the car. Someone else has taken the wheel"

Well you can believe me when I tell you that suddenly, none of us kids were tired anymore …

We were all in fear for our lives, as we watched Dad drive that car like there was no fog at all.

We passed cars that were in the slow lane, trundling along like snails, and obviously thinking that there must have been some kind of maniac driving our 375 Consul.

Dad said that, at that lowest moment, where we were fearing we wouldn't get home, he had suddenly felt a set of hands on top of his, holding the steering wheel.

He said they felt small, like ladies hands, and were cold.
At one point, he even let go of the steering wheel, and the car was driving itself. But Mum instantly made him put his hands back. And once again, the hands were back on his.

This continued for fifty miles or so, until we reached home.

And as we pulled up outside the house, and Dad switched the engine off, he felt the hands lift from his, and they were gone …

This has to be the creepiest journey we have ever experienced in our lives.

But whoever it was, they were there for our safety, and brought us home.

Dad always told Mum he thought it was his sister, my Aunty Louise.

It was easy to believe this, as this would be something that our special Angel would have done.

Dad could have said it was one of many people that had passed over, that helped us that night.
But his inner feeling from that moment on, was his sister.

As written by East Coast Angels:

This is a very common question in the paranormal field. As a paranormal researcher, I have read, heard stories, and studied this subject over and over again.

To be blunt, and pull no punches the answer is YES, a ghost, or spirit can follow a person home.
This doesn't mean that everyone will have a ghost as a stalker, or unwelcome guest.
It is very possible for a ghost to follow someone after they have had some kind of contact, or been in a haunted environment.
I say it is possible, not that it will happen, but it can.

I don't believe that there are ghosts just hanging around waiting to hitch-hike a ride with you.
There is a theory that a ghost or spirit may feel they have a kinship with a person.
A certain person may remind the ghost of a loved one, or spouse, or family member that they miss very much.
Most earthbound spirits, I believe are here because they are lost, or have some kind of unfinished business here on Earth.

My belief, is that it WAS my Aunty, and she had such love for us, she made sure we got home safely.

Incidentally, the car, that was in perfect condition, and had never had a problem at all . . . . . never started again……….

In traditional belief and fiction, a ghost (sometimes known as a Spectre (British English), or Specter (American English), phantom, apparition or spook) is the soul or spirit of a dead person or animal that can appear, in visible form or other manifestation, to the living.

Descriptions of the apparition of ghosts vary widely from an invisible presence to translucent or barely visible wispy shapes, to realistic, lifelike visions. The deliberate attempt to contact the spirit of a deceased person is known as necromancy, or in spiritism, as a séance.

The belief in manifestations of the spirits of the dead is widespread, dating back to animism or ancestor worship in pre-literate cultures.
Certain religious practices—funeral rites, exorcisms, and some practices of spiritualism and ritual magic—are specifically designed to rest the spirits of the dead.
Ghosts are generally described as solitary essences that haunt particular locations, objects, or people they were associated with in life, though stories of phantom armies, ghost trains, phantom ships, and even ghost animals have also been recounted.

A notion of the transcendent, supernatural or numinous, usually involving entities like ghosts, demons or deities, is a cultural universal. In pre-literate folk religions, these beliefs are often summarized under animism and ancestor worship.

In many cultures malignant, restless ghosts are distinguished from the more benign spirits involved in ancestor worship.

Ancestor worship typically involves rites intended to prevent revenants, vengeful spirits of the dead, imagined as starving and envious of the living.

Strategies for preventing revenants may either include sacrifice, i.e., giving the dead food and drink to pacify them, or magical banishment of the deceased to force them not to return.

Ritual feeding of the dead is performed in traditions like the Chinese Ghost Festival or the Western All Souls' Day. Magical banishment of the dead is present in many of the world's burial customs.

The bodies found in many tumuli (kurgan) had been ritually bound before burial, and the custom of binding the dead persists, for example, in rural Anatolia.

Nineteenth-century anthropologist James Frazer stated in his classic work, The Golden Bough, that souls were seen as the creature within, that animated the body.

Although the human soul was sometimes symbolically or literally depicted in ancient cultures as a bird or other animal, it appears to have been widely held that the soul was an exact reproduction of the body in every feature, even down to clothing the person wore. This is depicted in artwork from various ancient cultures, including such works as the Egyptian Book of the Dead, which shows deceased people in the afterlife appearing much as they did before death, including the style of dress.

A depiction of the ba, an element of the soul.

While deceased ancestors are universally regarded as venerable, and often imagined as having a continued presence in some sort of afterlife, the spirit of a deceased person which remains present in the material world, is regarded as an unnatural or undesirable state of affairs and the idea of ghosts or revenants is associated with a reaction of fear.
This is universally the case in pre-modern folk cultures, but fear of ghosts also remains an integral aspect of the modern ghost story, Gothic horror, and other horror fiction dealing with the supernatural.

It was December.
The night before my 16th birthday.

It was nearing Christmas, and excitement was building.

Growing up, I have to admit that Christmas was my favourite time of the whole year.

I could never put into words the joy that I felt, when I was old enough to help Mum decorate the Christmas tree.

Oh, we had always been allowed to participate in putting up the decorations, by making paper chains when we were younger.
I can still taste that vile gum you had to lick.
But it was the tree that always fascinated me the most. To this very day in fact. So as the holidays were drawing near, so was my feelings of excitement that another Christmas was almost upon us.

The early part of the year had been awful. In the Febuary.
My Dad's brother had died of a heart attack.
He was only 55 years old. And up to that point, he had been very healthy. He rode his bike everyday, didn't smoke, and kept himself in great shape.

He looked so much like my Dad, that sometimes people would get them mixed up. But they were also very alike in temperament too, and that stood to be a downfall. They had quick fiery tempers, and sometimes, speaking without thinking, would see them ignoring eachother for months on end.

Sadly, they were not talking at this particular point in time.

And neither one of them would back down and give in. So they certainly wouldn't be visiting one another, even though they lived in adjoining streets. Which makes the whole event very questionable as to whether my Uncle KNEW that he was going to die, because he turned up at our house, and knocked the door.

This was something he had NEVER done before, after an argument. Which was beyond strange within itself.

My Mum was getting ready for work, and opened the door.

The moment she saw my Uncle, she knew he was ill. In her words

"His face lit up the sky".

He was as white as a sheet, and he sheepishly asked if my Dad was home.

But he was at work, and Mum's mind was doing overtime, because she could see he wasn't well, and made him go into the house.

He was holding his chest, and said that it must be indigestion. At one point, he actually said "This pain is killing me ... There's a joke there somewhere" .....

Mum had always wanted to be a Nurse, and at this point, was pretty sure that he could be close to having a heart attack. If not already having one, or had one.

So she instantly made him lie down on the sofa, and put his feet up. This would have been unacceptable at any other time with my proud Uncle, which tells us how bad he must have felt, because he did what she asked.

In the meantime, Mum sent my brother to get my Auntie.

While he was lying down, with his feet up on cushions, and a little higher than his body, all the colour was coming back to his face, and his chest pain went away.

In this position, the blood can flow back to the heart properly, and was doing the trick long enough for his wife to arrive. Along with the Doctor.

He was checked over by the new Doctor that had just started at our surgery.

My Uncle said he thought it was indigestion, because of what he had eaten that morning, and that he was now feeling much better.

The Doctor prescribed indigestion medicine, and left.

During this time, my Uncle said as he was feeling better, he would make his way home.
My Mum suggested that he didn't ride the bike home, but that my Brother should take him in the car, and his wife would bring his bike home with her.
Under duress, he agreed.

My brother had only got to the top of the road, when suddenly, he was reversing at high speed back down the road again.

He said that Uncle had collapsed in the car. Everyone between them, carried him into the house as quick as they could, and laid him onto the floor.

They started CPR immediately, while the Doctor was rung again.

He hadn't even got back to the surgery when the call came through, so the other Doctor on call came straight out.

When he got to the house, he threw himself onto the floor, and carried on giving my Uncle CPR.

To no avail ......

My Uncle died on our floor, on that cold Febuary day.

Even the Doctor was in shock. Everyone was just stunned.

Nobody spoke. Nobody cried.

At the precise moment that he said he had "gone", the phone rang, and it was my Dad. He was ringing to say that he wasn't feeling very well, and that he was going to come home, because he had pains in his chest ....

Yes, that is how close they were. My Dad even felt his Brother's pain as he passed from this life.

Needless to say Dad was not told anything over the phone, except that his Brother had been taken ill, and best that he came home.

All this time, I had been in town with a friend, waiting to meet up with my Mum at work. When I had gone to see her, and was told she wasn't coming in, I had chills all over me.

 I knew when I left the house that all was fine, and she was getting ready to go.

So I ran all the way home, only to find the Doctor's car in the middle of the road with my Brother's, and my Uncle lying dead on the floor in our front room.

I will never forget that vision as long as I live.

I thought it was Dad lying there at first, until I noticed Uncle's Jacket and shoes.

No one was saying a word. The Doctor looked at everyone. He said we were all in shock. My Brother's heart was racing so fast, he had to give him something to slow it down.
He was in a terrible state.

No one was crying. Just still. Eerily still.

And then Dad walked in . . . .

I cannot put into words what happened that night, and the pain I see my Dad in, from the loss of his only Brother.
Those screams will stay with me to the end of my days.

But what I will say, is where my Uncle had been lying on the floor, a mark appeared on the carpet.

And to this day, we never knew what it was.
But no matter what we did, it would not go away . . . . . .

So ten months later, we are at the night before my birthday.

My Cousin was round, my Uncle's Son, and we were all sat round the fire talking about how we all missed him.
And Dad had got upset because they wasted so much time not talking, and was saying how much he regretted it.

I was sat there listening to all this, feeling very sad about everything.

I looked up at the clock, and see that it was coming up to midnight, and almost my birthday.

There was a silence in the room, as everyone was thinking about my Uncle.

So I suddenly said "Well if Uncle forgives us for not talking, he will come and wish me Happy Birthday tonight" ....

Dad said there was no doubt that my Uncle loved me.

I never said anything else, and soon after, I said goodnight to everyone, and went to bed....

There is always that element of "Why" when you wake up from a deep sleep in the middle of the night, for no apparent reason whatsoever.
And there is never a reason why, that you can see.

Tonight was different....

When I woke up, I was facing the wall.

I usually slept this way, with my back towards the door.
But this time, it felt different.

This time I was scared. This time, I felt like I wasn't alone.

And I knew in my heart that it wasn't my parents, or my Brothers.

The room was freezing cold.

Suddenly, I remembered it was my birthday.
And along with that memory, came the realisation of what I had said about my Uncle visiting me if he still loved me.

I don't know where I got the strength from, or how I fought the fear, but I made myself turn around...

And standing there, right by my bed, smiling, was my Uncle.

I froze.

I couldn't move.
I couldn't even shout for my Dad.
I was helpless.

I felt like I was laying inside a freezer, it was that cold.

But I couldn't take my eyes off of him.

He looked just as I remembered him. There wasn't a hair out of place as per usual. So very handsome.

But as I watched him smiling down at me, it seemed that I could see through him. Like he was only partly there.
It was really strange.

And as I lay there, scared for my life, he suddenly bent forward towards me, and came closer and closer. At this point, I thought I was going to die.

I closed my eyes. I just couldn't look no more.
I didn't know what was about to happen to me.
And I still had no voice to shout for Dad.

I squeezed my eyes shut, and waited for something terrible to happen....
I thought he was going to grab me, and take me with him.
My mind was doing overtime, and I was absolutely petrified.
But I still couldn't move. And I still couldn't scream.
I truly thought I was going to die ....

But instead, I felt, what I can only explain as, an ice cube touching my cheek.

It made my insides jump to high Heaven, and I instinctly opened my eyes, very wide no doubt.
Only to see my Uncle pulling away from my face, like he had kissed me.

He was stood upright again, filling my small room with all his glory.

He was still smiling. And then, without warning, he just faded away...

I was beside myself. I suddenly shivered profusely, trying to get a grip, and having trouble slowing down my heartbeat.

I STILL could not call, or go to Dad. I was overwhelmed. And to be honest, felt totally drained.

Then, slowly but surely, as I tried to make sense of what had just happened, the room began to warm up.

Within minutes, everything was back to normal.
My heart was still racing, but it had become bearable.

In this instance, I had run the whole experience over in my head, and sanity was telling me that it could have only been a good thing, and my Uncle, God rest his soul, had heard what I had said the night before, and had come to let me know that he did still love me.

Needless to say, I didn't go back to sleep for the rest of the night. And as soon as Dad woke up in the morning, I ran and told him what had happened.

He cried ....

Years later, I went to see a Psychic lady, who was known to be very good.

At this point, I had always believed that my Uncle and my Auntie were with me. There was nothing or no one that would make me believe otherwise.
But I wanted to see what she had to say.
She told me things that she couldn't have known.
Everything she said, was 100% correct.
I was so astounded by her.
I knew she was the real deal.
But she hadn't mentioned my "Angels".

Then, as she finished the session, she looked at me, with a wry smile, and said "You need to know something I haven't told you, don't you"? ...
"Yes" I said, looking directly into her very intense eyes.
"What is it you would like to know"?

I asked her immediately, if she knew of anyone that had passed over, but was with me.

Without hesitation, not only did she describe both of them, she gave me their names too ....

GUT FEELINGS ....
If you have them in your dreams or within your daily life, you may have the psychic gift. A gut feeling that is always accurate.
If you just "know" something before it happens, and you can sense the events of what is happening or what is about to happen, this is a strong sign of a psychic.

I have been told many times that I am psychic.
I sense things. I feel things. And I have seen things.
I truly believe within my heart, that I have this gift. And being brought up in a house that is full of *the other side* only deepens my belief.

A psychic is a person who claims to use extrasensory perception (ESP) to identify information hidden from the normal senses.
The word "psychic" is also used as an adjective to describe such abilities. Psychics may be theatrical performers, such as stage magicians, who use techniques such as prestidigitation, cold reading, and hot reading to produce the appearance of such abilities.
Psychics appear regularly in fantasy fiction, such as in the novel The Dead Zone by Stephen King.

Critics attribute psychic powers to intentional trickery or to self-delusion.

In 1988 the U.S. National Academy of Sciences gave a report on the subject and concluded there is "no scientific justification from research conducted over a period of 130 years for the existence of parapsychological phenomena.

A study attempted to repeat reported parapsychological experiments that appeared to support the existence of precognition.
Attempts to repeat the results, which involved performance on a memory test to ascertain if post-test information would affect it, "failed to produce significant effects", and thus "do not support the existence of psychic ability," and is thus categorized as a pseudoscience.

In a survey, reported in 1990, of members of the National Academy of Sciences, only 2% of respondents thought that extrasensory perception had been scientifically demonstrated, with another 2% thinking that the phenomena happened sometimes.
Asked about research in the field, 22% thought that it should be discouraged, 63% that it should be allowed but not encouraged, and 10% that it should be encouraged; neuroscientists were the most hostile to parapsychology of all the specialties.

A survey of the beliefs of the general United States population about paranormal topics was conducted by The Gallup Organization in 2005.

The survey found that 41% of those polled believed in extrasensory perception and 26% believed in clairvoyance. 31% of those surveyed indicated that they believe in telepathy or psychic communication.

A poll of 439 college students conducted in 2006 by researchers Bryan Farha of Oklahoma City University and Gary Steward of University of Central Oklahoma, suggested that college seniors and graduate students were more likely to believe in psychic phenomena than college freshmen. 23% of college freshmen expressed a belief in paranormal ideas. The percentage was greater among college seniors (31%) and graduate students (34%).

The poll showed lower belief in psychic phenomena among science students than social science and education students.

Some people also believe that anyone can have psychic abilities which can be activated or enhanced through the study and practice of various disciplines and techniques such as meditation and divination, with a number of books and websites being dedicated to instruction in these methods.

Another popular belief is that psychic ability is hereditary, with a psychic parent passing their abilities on to their children....

I believe it was passed on to me from my Mother.

My Mother, for as long as I can remember, has always had something *special*.

Would always know something was going to happen, before it did.

That "De Ja Vu" feeling, that we have all felt at some time or other in our lives, has nothing on my Mother.

She would know when someone was going to die in the family.

She would even know when there was going to be a plane crash!

How? You may ask.

In three words ... "In Her Dreams" ....

She even had a dream that she was going to meet Burt Lancaster, her favourite actor.

She dreamt that she was with him, talking to him. And what she remembered the most, and could see so clearly, was the bright red shirt he was wearing, and the wrist watch, with a black leather strap.

Three years later .... We met Burt Lancaster at the Savoy Hotel in London.

He was wearing a bright red shirt, and a wrist watch with a black leather strap ......

Mum once had a dream she was walking by the river, holding an empty basket.
It was late, and very dark in her dream. And she was scared, and crying.
She said out loud to herself "I wish my Dad was

here" ....
At this point, my Grandfather had been passed over around 20 years or so.
But, as Mum uttered these words in her dream, he was suddenly there, walking beside her.
She couldn't believe it.
"Dad, what are you doing here" !!!
And his simple answer was -
"You called for me" .....

Years later, my Mum's Sister went missing.
Nobody told us.
It was my Grandfather that once again, went to my Mum.
He woke her up, calling her name, in a very urgent manner.
And right there and then, Mum knew something had happened to her Sister.
That morning, sure enough, we found out she was missing.
We looked everywhere, but couldn't find her.
The days kept coming.
Friends and family became very worried, and were helping us to search for her.
Mum was fearing the worst, and in a terrible state.
We knew of a man that lived local, and was deemed a very good Psychic.
We were desperate at this point, so we contacted him.
He told us to go and see him.
So the following day, I went with Mum to see this gentleman.
We hadn't told him anything.
Not even our names.
We sat down, and immediately, he told Mum that she was looking for her Sister, and couldn't find her.
We just stared at him.

What an opener ....
Then he turned to my Mum and said -
"You think she's dead don't you" ?
Mum just nodded in agreement, trying not to cry.
"She's not dead. She's very much alive. On Sunday, the Police will knock at your door, and tell you they have found her".
He was so sure, we left there feeling the most optimistic we had, since her disappearance.
Needless to say, he was right.
The Police came on the Sunday. They took us to my Aunty, who didn't have a clue who she was, or where she was, and was in a terrible mess.
I cannot imagine the pain that she went through during those days, to end up like this.
She had been beaten so hard, she was left with brain damage.
And lived the rest of her life in a care home.
This beautiful soul, who wouldn't hurt a fly, was so independent, worked hard, and loved to travel, had been taken from us.
An evil monster took it all from her.
Someone that she loved and trusted implicitly.

Even now, I sit and wonder how bad things could have been, had my Grandfather not gone to Mum when he did.
Saving lives even from beyond the grave.
Saving the life of his youngest Daughter, who he taught to read and write, and clearly still felt her pain, and helped her.
Now she is buried with him. And no one can hurt her anymore ....

So NEVER be afraid to call for your loved one's, if you need them.
Ask for them to come to you.
BELIEVE.
Because they really are watching over us.
I am left with no choice but to believe, because of so many experiences in my life.
And although it was very frightening as a child, I have grown up thankful that I was able to be part of the "paranormal" that I truly witnessed.
I KNOW there is something after.
And that makes me feel warm in the knowledge that we WILL be with our loved one's again, albeit the pain we have to suffer when we lose them.
Remember, if you think you see something, or heard something -
You probably did !!
Don't fear them.
Embrace them.
Love them like you did on earth.
Because their love never stops ....

What is a psychic dream?
They certainly exist!

Precognition, also called prescience, future vision, future sight, is an alleged psychic ability to see events in the future.

As with other forms of extrasensory perception, there is no evidence that precognition is a real ability possessed by anyone and precognition is widely considered pseudoscience.

However, it still appears within movies, books, and discussion within the parapsychology community, with claimed precognition of earthquakes sometimes covered by the newsmedia.

Scientific investigation of extrasensory perception is complicated by the definition which implies that the phenomena go against established principles of science. Specifically, precognition would violate the principle that an effect cannot occur before its cause.
There are established biases affecting human memory and judgment of probability that sometimes create convincing but false impressions of precognition.

Belief in precognition has been related to superstition.

A 1978 Gallup poll found that 37% of Americans surveyed believed in precognition.

According to psychologists Tobacyk and Milford, belief in precognition was greater in college women than in men, and a 2007 Gallup poll found that women were more prone to superstitious beliefs in general.

A 2013 study discovered that greater belief in precognition was held by those who feel low in control, and the belief can act as a psychological coping mechanism.

An early inquiry into allegedly prophetic dreams was done by Aristotle in his "On Divination in Sleep".

His criticism of these claims appeals to the fact that "the sender of such dreams should be God", and "the fact that those to whom he sends them are not the best and wisest, but merely commonplace persons." Thus: "Most [so-called prophetic] dreams are, however, to be classed as mere coincidences...", here "coincidence" being defined by Aristotle as that which does not take "place according to a universal or general rule" and referring to things which are not of themselves by necessity causally connected. His example being taking a walk during an eclipse, neither the walk nor the eclipse being apparently causally connected and so only by "coincidence" do they occur simultaneously.

It is easy for people of science, to dismiss such things, if they have never experienced them. But what if they have?

It was understandable centuries ago, to keep things like that to yourself, because you would be burned at the steak for such witchcraft.

What of Nostradamus! he was a very lucky man, not to have left this world inside balls of fire.

Views on Nostradamus have varied widely throughout history.
At one end of the spectrum, there are extreme academic views such as those of Jacques Halbronn, who has suggested at great length and with great complexity that Nostradamus's Prophecies are antedated forgeries written by later hands with a political axe to grind.

At the other end of the spectrum, there are numerous fairly recent popular books, and thousands of private websites, suggesting not only that the Prophecies are genuine but that Nostradamus was a true prophet.

Due to the subjective nature of these interpretations, however, no two of them agree on exactly what he predicted, whether for the past or for the future. Many of these do agree, though, that particular predictions refer, for example, to the French Revolution, Napoleon, Adolf Hitler, both world wars, and the nuclear destruction of Hiroshima and Nagasaki. There is also an evident consensus among popular authors that he predicted whatever major event had just happened at the time of each book's publication, from the Apollo moon landings, through the death of Diana, Princess of Wales in 1997, and the Space Shuttle Challenger disaster in 1986, to the events of 9/11.

The prophecies retold and expanded by Nostradamus figured largely in popular culture in the 20th and 21st centuries.
As well as being the subject of hundreds of books (both fiction and nonfiction), Nostradamus's life has been depicted in several films and videos, and his life

and writings continue to be a subject of media interest.

A good living man, studying for his Doctorate in medicine, suddenly begins to dream of events in the future.

He sees buildings, planes, war, famine, murder, all things that haven't even happened. He sees the future!

I can only imagine how frightening that must have been for him.

In the 1500's, it wasn't natural! It wasn't the *done thing*, to tell people you can look into the future. But it overtook his life, and he leaned more towards the occult, than his studies of medicine. It engrossed him. Took over his mind.

I often wonder how I would feel if I were to have *dreams* of the future, on such a regular basis as he did. Would it send me crazy? Possibly.

But would I feel like I needed to tell people?

YES ! !

But centuries on, and we are still having to keep our *special* gifts to ourselves, for fear of ridicule, fear of isolation. And fear of being called crazy.

The media and their sceptics, certainly know how to keep us in line, that's for sure.

But it does happen.
People do have premonitions into the future.
I cannot explain it. I wouldn't like to try. But it happens.

It has happened to my own family. It has happened to me.
And I cannot just casually discard this, because Scientists cannot find any answer, other than superstition.
Or just pure mockery. Why? Because it hasn't happened to them ......

Evidence concludes that we only use 10% of our brain. What does anyone really know about the other 90% ? Do any of these Scientists really know the capabilities of every part of our brain? The extent of what it can achieve? Or where it can go while we are sleeping?
Many have said that they have actually left their body, and visitied other places, whilst lying in their beds. Other countries even.
Out of body* experiences.
Hovered above themselves during operations, and woke up and told the doctors exactly what they saw, and even what was being spoken about! But once again, only a scientific* explanation is given.
The findings showed that the conscious experience of where one's body is located arises from activity in brain areas involved in feelings of body ownership, as well as regions that contain cells known to be involved in spatial orientation, the researchers said. Earlier work done on animals, had showed that these cells, dubbed "GPS cells," have a key role in navigation and memory.

I totally agree that there are certain parts of our body that can react in the way the Scientists suggest, and a similar effect can be born.

But what of the experiences of one child that I was told about by his Father.

His Son was 5 years old. He was playing in his bedroom.
He went downstairs to his Mother, who was in the kitchen.
He told her he had just been to his Cousin's bedroom, and was playing with his train set.
His Mother, suddenly taken aback, asked him to repeat what he had just told her.

Not only did he describe what was in the room, but his Cousin lived in another country!

Well, as she was talking to him about it, the phone rang, and she went to answer it.

It was her Sister, calling from America.
She was in a state, and hard to understand.
When she finally was able to talk, she said she had just gone upstairs to her Sons bedroom, and seen her Nephew sat there with her Son's train set. And quickly rang to see if her Nephew was ok, because she thought something had happened to him, and she was seeing a ghost ......

Many strange things happened to this child whilst growing up, to the point where, now he is a man, he will not talk about it.
To anyone.
It has certainly had a profound effect on him. And his family obviously have never been able to understand how, or why these things happened to their Son.

So once again, we are left with unanswered phenomenon, and an open mind ....

I have NEVER asked a Scientist, or a Doctor, what they thought of this young child's experience.

Because no one wants to believe that such things can happen.

But they DO.

Can the body be transported to other places? Can we dream of events that haven't even happened yet? A look into the future? Are we living with the spirits of people who have passed to the other side?

There is only one answer in my book.

YES ....

My Dad was a very jealous man, when it came to Mum.

Oh, he was fine when it came to stopping for a chat in the street with friends. Or old school colleagues bumping into her, and stopping to reminisce while shopping in town.

As long as they were female ......

If she so much as smiled at, said hello, or passed the time of day with the male species, be it someone from school, a neighbour, or just a shopkeeper that kept the conversation going a little bit too long, he wouldn't like it.
Especially if they were good looking !!

And of course, Mum knew it too.

She would try her utmost when she was out, to avoid ANYONE that would trigger him off.

Even to the point of completely ignoring that person that had just said hello in passing.

But try as she might, it would never go un-noticed.

For the rest of the time they were out, Dad would go very quiet.

And we all knew what that meant.

Another night of Dad sulking, and his jealous rants.

The moment that front door was shut behind us, my Dad would find his voice.

And he wouldn't stop. .

You didn't bother him when he was in this mood, that's for sure.

And if you committed the cardinal sin, and answered him back for anything, you would regret it.

And all because my Mum said hello to an old school friend ....

Anyway, this could go on for hours sometimes.

And then, without warning, the silence would fall ...

He had had his rant. And now sat sulking, in another room.

My Mum of course, would be in tears, not liking these jealous outbursts at all.
Who would !

THIS, was one of those moments in time...

I was sat on the sofa with her in the front room.

She was very upset.

Dad had gone to the kitchen, to his *cooling off period*.

My brothers were out.

Mum had her face buried in her hands.

At that moment, I was just feeling thankful that peace had finally come, when my Mum suddenly said "Oh get off", and shrugged her shoulder, as if to move away from someone that had hold of her.

I said: "There's no one there Mum".

She looked behind her, expecting my Dad to be standing there, giving her his usual cuddle after being silly.

He wasn't.

He was still in the kitchen.

But he had heard her, and come through to the front room.

He said: "Who are you telling to get off? I wasn't anywhere near you".

My Mum looked very puzzled to say the least. And kept rubbing her left shoulder.

"Someone just put their hand on my shoulder" she said.

"Well it wasn't me" said Dad.

"But I felt it, as clear as anything" she said, and pulled down her top to look at her shoulder, and to show us where she felt the pressure of someone's hand.

Then came the shock .....

There was two distinct red lines on the top of my Mum's shoulder.

Now they wasn't just any old lines.

They formed a cross.... A perfectly shaped cross ....

It was overwhelming, to say the least.

And if that wasn't enough to be shocked about, what followed had me completely baffled.

After one of these *jealous* events, my parents wouldn't even speak to each other again, for hours. And then it would only be because they *had* to.

But, here they were, in full conversation, talking like they hadn't even had a cross word between them.

I couldn't understand it at all.

It had never happened before.

But then, Mum had never felt anyone put their hand on her shoulder before either, when there wasn't even anyone there for the eye to see....

And right after that, they sat and had a cup of tea together, discussing what had just happened, and then decided it would be a good idea to pop to the shops to get some groceries.

And off we went.
The calm, and the serenity in that house, was amazing.
Truly it was.
If that wasn't divine intervention, I don't know what is .....

During one of our many trips to London, to visit relatives, my Brother Colin decided that he was grown up enough now to be left at home!

He was a hard worker, and had got himself jobs as early as twelve years old, some of which were delivering newspapers, early in the mornings before school, and then he would help out in the town centre, selling clothes in the busy market place at the weekends.

He always took pride in himself, and would save his wages, and buy the shoes and clothes that were all the rave at the time, whether it be the Ben Sherman shirts, or the Loafer shoes that everyone wanted.

Colin would save hard, and get them.

Our Dad had brought us all up to make sure we could stand up for ourselves, should the occasion arise.

It wasn't as bad in the 70's ad 80's though, compared to now.

If you had a disagreement with someone at school, it would be a huge argument, a few days of ignoring eachother, and then it would be time to make up and be friends again.

With the boys, it would more than likely end up a fight in the playground, being sent to the Headmaster, or across the road in the park after school hours.

But even then, it would be over as soon as it started. And more often than not, the same two lads fighting hours before, would end up playing football together the same evening.

Unlike the days we live in now, where some people are even scared to walk to the local supermarket in the middle of the day, for fear of being mugged, beat up, or much worse.

So with Dad coming from a family, where his ancestors were street fighters, it was already in the blood, so to speak.
So he had his children, including myelf, training hard,

and learning Martial Arts throughout our childhoods. And some of us beyond.

And we loved every second of it.

So as you can imagine, by the time my brother had practically left school, there wasn't much that bothered him.
And he could certainly take care of himself, there was no doubt about that!

One of his friends, that lived down the road from us, was also into Martial Arts, and so their plan was, while we were all away in London, they would stay at our house, and have an evening of training at home.

After some time debating about it, my Dad finally agreed to let him stay.

And the following morning, we left home, minus a passenger.

As far as I can remember, my Brother had been out during the day, and his friend had come round to train with him that evening.

And up until this point, it had gone quite smoothly for them, having not hurt each other too badly, or broken anything in the house.

It was now getting quite late, and the evening was winding down.

The lads were practicing some *moves* in the front room, when suddenly, my Brother's friend stopped and said: "I thought you said the family had gone to London"?

"They have" said Colin, who at this point, was wondering what he meant.

"Then who is that walking around upstairs" ?

They both stood very still, and listened.

Above the front room, was the bedroom where my Brothers slept.

And someone was definitely walking across the floor up there.

Well, the first thing my Brother did, was look out of the window, to see if we had come home without him realising.
But the car wasn't outside.

"It's not them. The car isn't here"

Up until now, my Brother's friend, was the same as Colin.
Not scared of anything. Always trained hard, and took care of himself.

But at this point, he had never been told about the *events* that had always taken place in our house. So as you can imagine, the look on his face, and the fear in his eyes was something to see.

Before they had time to say anything else to each other, the footsteps had reached the top of the stairs, and began to climb slowly down, making a rattling sound like they were carrying something, or shaking something.

The footsteps came all the way down the stairs, very slowly, and meticulously.
And then they stopped.
Right at the bottom of the stairs, behind the door that led to the front room.
Other than stand there in the pose of Bruce Lee, waiting for the onslaught, they didn't know what else to do.
They were too frightened to open the door.
And then what seemed like forever, the footsteps started to make their way back up the stairs.
Just as slowly.
And just as meaningful.
It had just got to the top of the stairs, and began walking across the bedroom, from where it was first heard, when my Brother shouted "RUN", and they made a bolt for the front door, and out into the street.

And just as they reached the gate, we came round the corner, and pulled up outside the house.

Colin quickly told Dad what had happened, and Dad being Dad, went straight into the house.

He checked all the downstairs rooms, and there was no one there.
The back door was still locked.

He went upstairs, and checked every room.

And there was no one there either ....
Not that we expected anyone to be ....

As you can imagine, Colin didn't make a habit of staying at the house for the forseeable, whilst we were away.

And his friend also made other plans .....

The Victorians were haunted by the supernatural, by ghosts and fairies, table-rappings and telepathic encounters, occult religions and the idea of reincarnation, visions of the other world and a reality beyond the everyday.

Most Victorian poets had a strong opinion about the soul:
Elizabeth Barrett Browning, for instance, considered it the non-material counterpart of the fallen fleshly body, incompatible with material representation and only partially accessible to consciousness.

As written by Kira Cochrane:-
Christmas Eve was traditionally the time to tell scary stories round the hearth.
And 19th-century writers were fearsomely adept at exploiting a world of creaking floorboards, creepy servants … and gas lamps that caused hallucinations.
Curl up by the fire and I'll tell you a ghost story.
Don't be alarmed by the creak of the floorboards, the murmurs in the basement, the shrill ululations of a distant dog.
Try not to be perturbed by the flickering candle, the

fleeting shadows, the horned, hairy hand that appears at your elbow. Something moved?
There's a face in the brickwork?
A murderer, long ago, was buried in the cellar?
Stay calm. Breathe deeply.
The ghosts of Christmas past are gathering....

So ... Not much different 200 years on then !!!!
Some people still frightened of the dark, and what it may bring.
Some still afraid of seeing spirits, wailing through the night.
While others, welcome the idea to actually have the chance to catch up with a passed soul.
The world is still, and I'm sure, will always be, frightened of the *after life*, or the actual fear of making the acquaintance of a phenomenon that doesn't belong to this world.
I can certainly understand, when a person has had no such experiences from beyond the grave, and remain sceptical.

It stands to reason when they have seen nothing, and keep their minds closed.

One survey in 2017 found, in fact, that around a third of people living in England, believe in ghosts, with even the most sceptical of us often spooked by unexplained bumps in the night.

So what is it about ghosts that has captured our imagination for so many centuries?
And is there a rational explanation for why sightings are so common?
For sceptics – or scaredy-cats looking for some comfort – here are some of "science's" best guesses:-

VERBAL SUGGESTION AND THE POWER OF BELIEF
Simple yet effective, several studies have shown that people are more likely to report a location as being haunted if it's been suggested to them that it is. This kind of suggestion is also the way that a lot of "psychics" operate.
It's also been suggested that the power of our will is much stronger than we might think – and simply wanting to see a ghost might be powerful enough to create an impression of one.

ELECTROMAGNETIC FIELDS
Michael Persinger, a Canadian neuroscientist, has studied the effect of electromagnetic fields on people's perception of "ghosts".

He hypothesises that pulsed magnetic fields – which we can't detect on a conscious level – can cause unusual activity patterns in the brain's temporal lobes and lead to people perceiving a "presence" in a room.

Though there has been some pushback against his theory, other scientists have found that places with a reputation for being haunted – like Hampton Court –

do have unusual magnetic fields.

MOULD
(Growing inside homes, giving off fumes that cause hallucinations)

CARBON MONOXIDE POISONING
(Causing hallucinations)

OUIJA BOARDS
(The ideomotor effect - Which apparently, is an example of involuntary, unconscious physical movement, and is a way for our bodies to speak to themselves without us being aware.

When using a Ouija board, users will often unconsciously have messages that they want to receive when asking questions to a "spirit." This means our body responds to our brain's unconscious desires and moves our hand without conscious input - giving the impression that it's being controlled by external forces ....

I guess there is nothing wrong with sceptics, and scientists, trying to blow away any notion that there could actually be life after death.
After all, for most, if you can't see it, then it isn't there right?

But what of the people that do see it?
And have no mould, or carbon monoxide poisoning?
Or verbal suggestions, power of belief, electromagnetic fields, or a Ouija board in their house?
What would these same *sceptics* say, if they were actually present at the wailings of a poltergeist?
And they knew categorically that none of the above existed within the haunting?

What would they put it down to then?
Hysteria?
Someone has drugged them?
I'm sure the excuses would be endless, and they could roll out numerous *scientific* reasons why they experienced such a haunting.
But when you have grown up in a home, where it happened over and over again, and spirits even followed you OUT of that home, eventually, you have to resort to the fact that these happenings are REAL. And they are happening to YOU.
Thankfully, times have moved on somewhat, and hauntings and such like are actually discussed, despite science trying to discredit each and every one of them.
I guess that beats being thrown into an asylum on the grounds of lunacy right?
All I can say is, thank goodness I was born when I was.
Or I could have spent the rest of my days being doped, and confined to a small room, and left to deal with my experiences alone, and un-believed ...

When my Dad's Sister passed, in the most horiffic way, it was sadly down to my parents to go around to her home where she had lived, and clear out her belongings.
As you can appreciate, this was a very hard thing to do, as they had been so close to her, and loved and missed her very much.
But her partner (We will call him Josh), had left the home, and wouldn't go back, because two days after she died, the lights just kept blowing in every room he walked in.
Ornaments kept moving of their own accord.
But the electric fire blowing up, was the straw that broke the camel's back.
He left.
Very quickly.

He asked my parents to do it for him...

I remember so vividly, walking through town with Mum and Dad, on our way to my Auntie's home.
We had got to the middle of the square, and was heading for the arcade to cut through, when suddenly, what seemed like a voice from above us, called my Father's name.
All 3 of us stopped in our tracks.
The voice called him again ....
The square was absolutely full of men, women, and children, bustling around, walking in all directions, on their way home, shopping, or just sat on the seats watching their children feeding the birds.
Nobody looked our way.
Not one.
That voice was so loud to us, and so clear.
Yet we were the only one's that heard it.
It came from above, yet seemed behind us.
It was a woman's voice.
A familiar voice.
By the second time we heard her call my Father, we knew it was the voice of my dead Auntie calling him.
Without a shadow of a doubt.
It sounded urgent.
Like she was really trying to get my Father's attention.
Mum suddenly had a thought.
From where we heard the voice coming from, there was a pub.
A pub, that her partner Josh would frequent.
Mum suddenly said "I bet she is trying to tell us that he is in the pub and not at the house".
It seemed the perfect answer.
So we went over to the pub.
And there was Josh .... Having a drink, frightened for his life.
He said he could feel her with him where ever he was, and it was so strong, it was scaring him.

My parents tried to calm him down for a while.
And eventually, they took the keys from him, and went and cleared the house for him.
Josh never went back there again.
He drank himself to death only a few years later, and was found in the back garden of an empty house, lying in the barn.
He just didn't want to live without her anymore ....

But yeah .... I guess that was all down to hallucinations, mould, carbon monoxide, electromagnetic fields, and ouija boards ......

When someone has dreams, psychic ability, or that sixth sense within them, like my Mother, to predict future events, sometimes it can "change" the outcome for the better, that's for sure.

One day, my brother Colin came round, and asked my parents if they wanted to go for a drive with him.
He had to pick something up from his boss, and it was out of town.
Mum and Dad wasn't busy, it was a lovely afternoon, so they went along for the ride.
Colin headed off, and it wasn't long before they had almost reached the small village on the outskirts of town, where his boss lived.
But as they got closer, Mum asked my brother what the name of the village was.
He told her, and she looked very puzzled.
Dad asked her what was wrong, and she said that everything started to look familiar to her. Yet it was a place she had never been to in her life!
As they got closer, Mum began to tell Dad and my brother what was going to be around the corners they were driving up to.
And each time, she was correct.
At this point, Mum was beginning to panic.
It was all coming back to her.

A few months before this particular day, Mum had had one of her "dreams".
And in this dream, the events had unfolded exactly the same way.
My brother had asked them if they wanted to go for a ride with him.
To the very same village, to see his boss.
The village was exactly as it was in her dream.
But the next part of the dream was the bad part.
Because Mum said when they reached the house of my brother's boss in her dream, my Dad went with him, and Mum had waited in the car for them.
But as it was a nice day, and they were taking a while, she had decided to get out of the car, and just go for a walk across the way, where there were some lovely fields and walkways.
She came up to a path that seemed to cut through the field, and decided she would just walk down it a little way.
As she did this, suddenly, from nowhere, a really huge man, with a monstrous face, stepped out in front of her, and went to grab her.
She screamed, and turned to try and get away from him.
And at this point, she woke up in a complete panic.
I remember her telling us about this dream the next day.
We hadn't really spoken about it since, and it had been forgotten about.
Until now ....

"The road where your boss lives, is going to be round this next corner Colin" she said, when they arrived in the village.
 And went on to tell him exactly which house it was.
She was absolutely correct.
"You're not going in with him" she said to my Dad.
"You can stay here with me" !
Well Dad totally understood her fear, and of course, waited in the car with her.

While they were waiting, they decided to take that walk, because Dad was a big man, and now Mum had him by her side, she wasn't so scared of the bogey man. Sure enough, they came to the path by the field, and began walking down it.
But no very huge monster faced bogey man jumped out at her.
But Dad was on his guard, just in case !
However, My Mum did say that she could feel someone watching her, and knew without a doubt, that if she hadn't of had that dream, and gone down the path alone, it would have surely happened, and she would have been face to face with him ....

Overwhelming proof that we can change the route our lives are on, if we have that extra special gift to be able to do it.
Overwhelming proof that Mum could see into the future, and was able to change it for the better.
And overwhelming proof, that she wasn't crazy, like they would have had us believe years ago, when they would shut people away for saying such things. She dreamt of a place she had never visited before in her life, and yet knew every part of it.
Knew what was round every corner.
And in doing so, was thankfully able to save herself from what could have been a very different ending to a lovely sunday afternoon drive with her Son .....

Mum and Dad slept in the bedroom that overlooked the back garden.
I remember one particular day so vividly, as children, when me and my brother Phillip were poorly, and couldn't go to school.
Dad was at work, and we were home with Mum.
It was winter time, and the colds and stomach bugs were doing their rounds as usual.
That house was so cold in the winter.
There was no luxury of radiators and gas fires in those days !
But we did have a fireplace in 2 of the bigger bedrooms.
And I remember Mum had lit the fire, and put us in her bed.
It was lovely and warm in there.
She had given us comics to read, and we had our drawing books too.
I can see it now - Phillip was doing a sketch of one of the characters from his comic. And I was colouring in a picture of a little girl, standing around a Christmas tree in her front room, with a dog by her side, and so many pretty decorations, on the ceiling, and on the tree.
As I sit here remembering - I can almost smell the fireplace, and the distinct aroma of Lucozade, that we had in our glasses to drink.
Dad swore by it, and always made sure we had a bottle for such times when we were ill.

To this day, I have no idea why that particular memory stays with me.
But it always has.
And makes me feel warm inside, just thinking back.
I'm guessing it was because at that moment in time, although we were off school sick, we were at home, warm, and safe with Mum.
Safe' being the operative word.

It was daytime, and Mum's bedroom was my special *safe*

place, especially when I would be scared during the night, sleeping in a room on my own, but would be allowed to get in with Mum and Dad and sleep soundly again, knowing there was no chance of anyone getting to me between my two most favourite people in the world !
And Mum and Dad always made us feel so safe.
I can still remember the flowers on the wallpaper. And most of all, the dressing table Mum had in there, with a big mirror in the middle, that I so often use to stand in front of, trying on Mum's clothes and shoes, and playing with the ribbons in my hair.
I must have stood in front of that mirror a thousand times .....
My safe room. My security blanket.
My special place ....

Unfortunately, it wasn't the case for Mum as it turned out .....

I would say I must have been around 10 years old at the time.
We had all gone to bed, and the house was in silence. The dog was lying at the top of the stairs, as he always did, because even he wouldn't stay down there on his own at night.
And all was well with the world.
Or so we thought ....

Mum woke up for no reason whatsoever.
She was lying in bed, facing Dad.
But the more she became awake, the more she felt like there was someone else in the room with them.
Dad was sound asleep, and not stirring at all.
Mum was becoming quite fearful, because she had an overwhelming sensation that someone was behind her, at the side of the bed.

She knew from the coldness that was in the room, something wasn't right.
She also knew that it wasn't going to be one of us kids either, because we would never walk round that side of the bed if we needed anything.
Dad slept nearest the door, and we would always wake him up.
The longer she lay there, the more scared she became.
And the more scared she became, the more she couldn't move.
Then came the noise ....
The only way Mum could explain it to us, was that it sounded like a *chomping* sound, like teeth clicking together.
And it was coming from behind her.
In her panic, she just had to look around to see what it was.
And she wished to God that she hadn't ....
A skeleton was stood by her bed, chomping it's teeth at her.
And as she looked around, it started shaking it's arms and rattling it's bones.
And it wouldn't stop.
She was absolutely petrified.
But she couldn't scream.
She threw the covers over her head, and tried to wake my Dad.
Now my Dad would wake with the slightest sound.
ALWAYS.
He was a very light sleeper.
That night, my Mum shook him. She called his name.
She resorted to pinching him so hard, he had bruises the next day.
But she could not wake him.
And so she lay under the covers, shaking like a leaf, absolutely petrified that this skeleton was going to grab her.
But she could not move. Her legs had gone, and her body had turned to jelly.

She laid like that for what seemed like an eternity, praying that it would go away.
 And eventually - It did.
The *chomping* stopped.
The bones stopped rattling.
The room was warm again. And she knew it had gone.
And right at that moment, Dad miraculously woke up.
She quickly told him what had happened, but it was too late.
Whoever it was *chomping* their bits, had gone...

To this very day, My Mum cannot talk about it, without shuddering, or quickly changing the subject.
Her facial expression says it all. It was horrendous for her.
It was the worst thing that ever happened to her in that house.
I really don't know what I would have done, if that had of been me.
I think I would have just collapsed.
Just the thought of it, chills my blood.
I doubt you could call that a "nice" visit from the other side.
But I guess there's good and bad in all walks of life AND death ...
There will always be a reason for a "nice" visit, or a not so nice one.
If we think hard enough, logic will tell us that we have done something to deserve it, either way, or, it could be someone that once lived in that very home, has nothing to do with the family, or the person, but feels the place still belongs to them, and wants it back.
It could be an upset relative, or a friend, absolutely anyone.
The list is endless.
So it would be very hard to pinpoint why such things take place sometimes.
And understandably why so many people are fearful of

the unknown.
Mum thinks she knows "who" it was, and "why" that particular visitor came that night.
And although they wasn't there to hurt anyone, there really isn't any solace in experiencing a skeleton shaking it's bits at you is there ...

As you can imagine, it was a while before she could sleep properly again.
Needless to say, she didn't sleep on that side of the bed anymore ......

A ghost is the soul or spirit of a dead person or animal that can appear to the living.
In ghostlore, descriptions of ghosts vary widely from an invisible presence to translucent or barely visible wispy shapes, to realistic, lifelike forms.
The deliberate attempt to contact the spirit of a deceased person is known as necromancy, or in spiritism as a séance.
Other terms associated with it are apparition, haunt, phantom, poltergeist, shade, specter or spectre, spirit, spook, wraith, demon, and ghoul.

The belief in the existence of an afterlife, as well as manifestations of the spirits of the dead, is widespread, dating back to animism or ancestor worship in pre-literate cultures.
Certain religious practices—funeral rites, exorcisms, and some practices of spiritualism and ritual magic—are specifically designed to rest the spirits of the dead.

Ghosts are generally described as solitary, human-like essences, though stories of ghostly armies and the ghosts of animals rather than humans have also been recounted.

They are believed to haunt particular locations, objects, or people they were associated with in life. According to a 2009 study by the Pew Research Center, 18% of Americans say they have seen a ghost.

A place where ghosts are reported is described as haunted, and often seen as being inhabited by spirits of deceased who may have been former residents or were familiar with the property.

Supernatural activity inside homes is said to be mainly associated with violent or tragic events in the building's past such as murder, accidental death, or suicide—sometimes in the recent or ancient past. However, not all hauntings are at a place of a violent death, or even on violent grounds. Many cultures and religions believe the essence of a being, such as the 'soul', continues to exist.

Some religious views argue that the 'spirits' of those who have died, have not 'passed over,' and are trapped inside the property where their memories and energy are strong.

All I can tell you, is the house I grew up in, was blessed by a Priest.
My parents actually tried this.
But nothing changed.
I truly believe that a certain place can be the home of wandering spirits, crying out in the night.
I have no choice but to believe this, given that I experienced so much of it in the house I grew up in, during the first 18 years of my life.
You can certainly try brushing these events aside, if you feel that you could have *imagined* it.
But you can only *imagine* so many times before you

actually begin to question what in the world is going on, as they happen over and over again.

But I also believe, that it can be due to the person, or people, that the spirits are coming back to visit, and not necessarily the place they are living in.
If a person is suddenly snatched away from life, and not ready to leave loved one's, I honestly feel that, for one reason or another, they do not *cross over* like other people do, when they have lived their lives, and ready to go to rest.
They are clinging on for their unlived days.
Trying to stay among us.
Not ready to leave for all eternity.
They are taken from their bodies all too soon, and all too sudden, and the spirit and the soul tries to fight against it.
And if the will is strong enough, they clearly succeed ...

I once told a friend about the times when things went bump in the night at our old house.
She had lost her Husband, and had never had any, shall we say, further communciation from him, after he passed away.
Sometimes, you have to be careful who you confide in with such things.
I honestly thought she would understand, which was why I told her in the first place.
I thought she was a believer.
But I guess there are some people we meet in life, that really disappoint us, when it comes to our faith in them.
I thought I knew her.
I clearly didn't.
She laughed.
And then replied with - "Don't be silly. It's just a case of mass hysteria" ...
Hmm ..... *Mass Hysteria* ...

Mass Hysteria refers to apparently contagious dissociative phenomena that takes place in large groups of people or institutions under conditions of anxiety......
 So when you are sat in a room with a visitor, drinking a cup of tea, and your Dad's shoes pick themselves up in front of everyone, and drop to the floor again, I guess that was *Mass Hysteria* ...
And I guess when you're minding your own business, sleeping, in the middle of the night, and you are woken by a dead relative standing by your bed, or playing games in front of the fire with your children, and an ash tray is thrown at you by invisible hands, and smashes into a thousand pieces, it's *Mass Hysteria* ....
Somehow, I don't think so !
There were certainly never *large groups of people* during these trying times, that's for sure.
And if the truth be said, I think I can safely say, that *anxiety* wasn't a factor either. Only after the events !
We were hardly anxious playing Ludo on a blanket ......

Again, you do have to be careful who you talk to, when it comes to something as complex as the *other side*, should you experience it in this life.

Choose your audience wisely ..

Before my Uncle died in our house, we had so many happy memories with him over the years.
He would always come round of an evening, and spend many hours with Dad, just chatting away about anything and everything.
They were so alike in their ways. But sometimes, that was a set back, because they both had very bad tempers, as I told you earlier.
And believe me when I say, it didn't take a lot to

trigger them either ...
I think I can safely say their biggest bugbear, between them, were the school teachers !
As a lot of you may be old enough to remember, corporal punishment wasn't a rarity back in the day.
And many felt the wrath of a headmaster's cane, or an English teacher's slipper, getting 6 of the best in front of the other children.
Or even a good aim with the board rubber, that would come hurtling across the room from an angered teacher.
They didn't have a lot of patience with the kids that's for sure.
And they made it known. Regularly...
Neither my Dad, or my Uncle, would stand for their children to be smacked by anyone other than themselves, if the children were naughty.
They came from a family of fighters, and hardened farm workers, that would always put their families first, no matter what.
And if anyone felt that they could mess with that, then it was down to them to face the consequences.
If any *smacking* went on at the schools we were all going to, then Dad and Uncle would be over there, and deal with the situation.
Most teachers, because they had *heard* that it wasn't a good idea to hurt any of my family members, found other ways of punishing.
Usually ending up with lines, staying late after school, or being reprimanded in front of everyone in assembly.
But there were always going to be the odd few, that thought they were tough enough, that they could get away with it.
It was always bound to happen.
I have to say, that out of the two of them, Dad was the more frightening though.
I will never forget when my brother Colin was baited by some of his school friends, to throw a stone over the fence, into the school swimming pool.

Well my brother wasn't going to back down, and he did that very thing.
Unfortunately, one of the boys that see him do it, ran and told on him, and sure enough, my brother was sent to the headmaster.
He gave Colin a good telling off that day, and my brother said sorry for doing wrong.
But it wasn't enough.
The headmaster pulled out a cane from his desk, and told Colin to hold out his hand.
As he went to hit his hand, Colin ducked his arm back, and he missed.
He told him to hold out his other hand, and he done the same thing again.
What proceeded after that, should never have happened. Not to any child.
My brother was set upon by this man, who was so enraged that Colin had ducked his hand away twice, that he just hit him over and over and over again, all around his body, until my brother couldn't take it any more.
He ran out of the office, and all the way home.

It took many Police officers to pull my Father off of that headmaster, for what he done to my brother.
By the time Colin had got home after that beating, his body had so many lumps and bruises all over it, even the Police officer that came to the house, said he would have done the same as my Father.
It was disgusting.
To the point that my parents were offered the chance to have the headmaster sacked from his position at the school.
And possibly any other school after that.
But they didn't do it. As far as they were concerned, he got his just deserves, and they let him keep his job.
I'm sure he was forever thankful for that, and certainly didn't hit any child to that extent afterwards.

My parents received a letter from him, apologising profusely, and thanking them.
In fact, my Mum still has that very letter in her possession, all these years later.
And when I eventually was old enough, and went to the same school, that headmaster could not have been any nicer to me !
Mind you, I wasn't naughty at school. I loved school, and was too scared to get in trouble, because I knew I would have to answer to Dad !
But I became one of this headmaster's favourite pupils, and would regularly get his dinner, and even sit with him having mine.
And when Christmas came around, and he would be in the dining room, cutting the Christmas pudding (something he did every year), when he see it was me, he would always make sure that I had a threepenny bit in my pudding !
I loved him very much to be honest.
He always praised me, and gave me good reports.
And I was in touch with him, even after he retired, and moved down to the seaside with his wife.
I was very sad when he passed away.
But I always wonder just how awful a person he could have become, had he not felt the wrath of my Father.
I think it actually saved him.
And his career.

And of course, this was the same for my Uncle. Many a time, he had to be removed from the school, because he had lost his temper, because of teachers thinking they can do what they want to his children.
He just wasn't going to have it.
Just like Dad.

But those of us that knew and loved my Uncle, also see the soft side to him.
One time in particular, that will always stay with me, was when I was at home poorly with tonsilitis,

and feeling very sorry for myself.
He had come round to see Dad.
Now, it didn't matter where you see him, or whether he was at home, at your house, or in the street, Uncle always had a packet of mints on him.
I believe they were called Pacers if I'm not mistaken. And he would always be sucking on one when he came through the door at our house.
I loved the smell of them. In fact, to this very day, when I smell mint, it reminds me of him.
He felt sorry for me this day, and took out his mints and gave one to me.
Which was a bit of a shock to be fair, because he hadn't done it before !
However, I thanked him, and got up to give him a cuddle.
At this point, he said to me "stand on my shoes".
I was around 10 years old, and not very big, and he lifted me a foot off the floor, and put my feet back down on top of his.
He grabbed my hands and started dancing with me around the room.
I loved it !!
Dad and Mum were laughing. And so was my Uncle.
I didn't want to stop ! No one had ever done that before.
And it became a regular thing after that.
Every time he came round, he would give me a mint, and I would dance on his shoes with him.
Lovely memories ...

And they did just become memories, when he died in our house on that fateful cold, febuary day, 5 years later.
It was heartbreaking losing him.
Especially for Dad.
We had lost our Grandmother the year before, and Uncle had said more than once to Dad, that he missed her so much, and that he would be next to go, and he would be with her again.
My Dad use to tell him off for talking that way.

But he continued to say it.
"I know I'm going to be next" he would say.
Maybe another family member, that had the sixth sense.
Sadly, he was right ....

That year, we struggled through his loss. My Dad trying hard to come to terms with the fact that his only brother had gone.
He missed their evening chats so much, he cried regularly.
It was awful.

While my Uncle was still alive, he would ride his bike everywhere.
Some have said that the couple of miles he cycled the morning he came to ours, and died in our house, had probably kept his heart beating that little bit longer.
He loved that bicycle.
My eldest brother Kenneth, was very close to my Uncle. They use to talk regularly, usually about fixing cars and vans, as it was a passion for both of them.
And many a night, when my brother was parked outside his fiancee's house saying goodnight, Uncle would ride past, coming from his Sister's house, tap on my brother's car roof, and shout out "Goodnight Kenneth".
My brother would shout goodnight back to him, and he would wave, and carry on home, not to disturb them.
This became the *norm*.
Uncle always seemed to time it right, that they would be saying goodnight most evenings.
And the year we had lost him, wasn't any different .....

My brother had been affected deeply, with the loss of Uncle, because he actually collapsed in my Brother's car to begin with, and everyone had to carry him into our house, and call for help.
It had been a terrible ordeal for Kenneth.

It must have been a few months after Uncle died.

Kenneth was sat outside of his fiancee's house, in the car, and they were having their last chat of the evening, before they said goodnight.
And suddenly, out of the blue, was the tap on the roof of the car, and my Uncle's voice shouting "Goodnight Kenneth" .....
It was as loud, and as real as it could sound.
My brother and his fiancee were, as you can imagine, absolutely rooted to the spot.
I'm sure if she hadn't of heard it aswell, he would have thought he imagined the whole thing.
Their hearts were thumping.
They could not believe what had just happened.
They even heard the bike !!
But they couldn't see a thing ...
And it never happened again ...

Maybe it was Uncle's special goodbye to one of his favourite's.
We may never know.
But it was very special for my brother.
And it didn't take long, before he let us know he was still around again ...

I remember this night so vividly. Like it was yesterday
There was just myself, Mum, and my Cousin at home.
It was dark outside, and we were in the front room, just having a cup of tea and a chat.
Like any other evening.
My Cousin was one of those people that found it hard to believe in something that he cannot see or feel.
And he found it hard to believe in God.
And certainly didn't believe in ghosts that romed the earth.
I often wonder if I hadn't of had so much happen to me growing up, whether I would have been the same as most sceptics.
But I do feel that I would have been more open minded to it at least.

But I can only imagine how hard it is, for someone to believe in such things, if they have never had any experience of it.
However, my Cousin had always known about the things that had happened to us, and was about to have his eyes opened ....

We had just been talking in general. Nothing in particular.
And certainly wasn't talking about Uncle passing.
All of a sudden, we all stopped talking.
And we listened. Even my Cousin.
It was around 10pm in the evening, and very dark outside.
Usually the time that my Uncle would have come round to see Dad.
He would come through the gate with his bicycle, walk it up the path, and put it under the sill, and tap the window.
We always knew it was Uncle. And always around the same time.
And this night was no different. Apart from the fact that he had already died that is ...
Because we had been talking, the tv wasn't on, and so you could hear anything that was going on outside the window.
No one said a word.
When the sound of the bicycle came up the path, and clearly parked under the sill of the front window, Mum said she knew straight away who it was.
And she was waiting for the window to be tapped.
And sure enough, there it was. The rapping on the window, from somebody's hand.
All 3 of us knew this was what Uncle had always done. Including my disbelieving Cousin.
Without hesitation, he jumped up, and quickly opened the front door.
There was nobody there. He walked around to the back of the house.

Nothing.
Looked up and down the street.
Nothing.
The moment the tap on the window had come, my Cousin was so quick to open the front door, that if it had been anyone of this world, they couldn't have got away quick enough.
Let alone rode off on the bike without being heard.
Well ... He came back in the house, and just looked at us, dumbfounded.
I don't think he could actually believe that he had been witness to it.
He had heard it as clear as us. And yet there was no one, or nothing there.
It's safe to say that even he had to admit something strange had happened that night.
And all credit to him, he never tried to deny it either.
And we have often spoken about it over the years.

Sometimes, even the sceptics have to concede to the other side,
whether they want to, or not .....

Speaking with my Mum the other day, and reminiscing about the good old days, we did inevitably, turn our attentions to the "bad old days", as we have on so many occasions over the years.
My Son was with me.
And was listening profusely, as he was told about the happenings that took place in our lives, from his Nan, who lived every part of it as much as I did, possibly more I would imagine.

And as Mum was describing different events to him, and clearly showing the emotions that were still so clearly in her mind, like it was yesterday, she suddenly started talking about something that I had completely put to one side over the years.
So, as you can imagine, it has been very hard recalling all the awful memories, after such a long time, and try to put them into words, without the pain returning.
I have always tried to do that - Put bad memories to one side, if they had a very negative effect on me.
This was one of those memories ...

I would have been around 12 years old at the time.
It was in the middle of summer, with us children off school for the holidays.
There was just me and Mum at home.
Dad was at work, and the boys were off out doing their thing.
I was helping Mum to bring the washing in, that had been drying on the line.
I remember the old lady so clearly, that lived next door to us whilst I was growing up.
She was one of those people, that you were petrified of, with just receiving one of her angry stares that she so often gave.
You did not want to be the one to have to knock her door, and ask if you could please have your ball back, as it had been kicked over the fence.
Sometimes, my brothers, as they got older, would just leap over and grab it, and jump back onto our side pretty quickly, before she had time to look out of the window.
She ALWAYS seemed to be peering out of that kitchen window of hers.
She couldn't have had that much washing up to do at the sink surely to goodness.
But it didn't matter what time of day we were in the back garden, we would look up, and sure enough, there

she was, peering over the top of the low hung net curtain, with a face that could turn the milk sour.
The only one's that didn't seem to be scared of her, were her cats !
And she had a few of them as I recall.
The one that followed her everywhere, was the black & white Tom cat she had.
If she was putting her washing out, the cat was by her feet.
If she was sat on the step, the cat was beside her.
And would you believe it, whenever she would be at the kitchen sink, peering out of that window, that very same cat would jump onto her shoulder, and just sit there.
He absolutely idolised her.
None of the cats would go to anyone else, if you tried to coax them, or get close enough to stroke them.
They would just run away, or run back into the house.

I am pretty sure I never ever see that old lady smile.
Not once.
In all the years I lived next door to her.
Even her own Son wasn't keen on visiting.
He was totally different to her.
He was friendly with Mum & Dad, and always had a smile to give, or a kind word to the neighbours when he was visiting.
So it clearly wasn't just me and my brothers that found her hard to be around. And as I recall, there wasn't any other neighbours that were friendly with her either.

So this is my memory of the old lady next door.
And it never changed.

I remember lying in bed one night. It was getting very late, and as per usual, I was struggling to sleep in that house.
But there was a tap on the front door.

I found out afterwards, that it was a passing neighbour who had knocked.
And when we opened the door, they were walking away, but signalled to my Mum to look next door.
Mum stepped out of the front door, and saw that the old lady was stood on her front step, seemingly very poorly, and needing help.
Mum being the wonderful lady that she is, quickly helped her inside, and laid her down on the sofa.
She was so ill, she could hardly talk.
So Mum made her as comfortable as she could, and told the old lady she was going to call the doctor for her, and would come back.
Back in those days, nobody had a house phone.
So Mum threw her coat on, and ran to the nearest phone box that was three streets away.
She called the doctor, and he came quickly. (They did in those days).
The ambulance arrived, and took the old lady to hospital.

It was about a week later. The old lady's daughter knocked our door.
We rarely saw her, as she lived out of town.
She came to tell us that her Mum had passed away in hospital, but that before she died, she had told her how my Mum had helped her, and wanted to thank her.
So although very sad, that was a lovely thing to hear at the time.
My Dad went and found her Son, and sadly gave him the bad news.

It was about two weeks later, after the old lady had passed away, that me and Mum were in the back garden, bringing in the washing.
Mum was unpegging it from the line, and I was putting it into the basket.
And as I was waiting for the next bit of clothing, I happened to think of the old lady, and looked over

at her kitchen window.
I wish I hadn't ....
I had to do a double take. I looked away, and looked back.
And sure enough, I was right the first time.
There the old lady was. Peering through the net curtain I whispered to Mum in a very scared voice, to look up at her window.
And as we both looked up, and this was the part that really was unforgettable, that same black & white cat jumped onto the shoulder of a woman that had been dead for two weeks, and buried in the graveyard across town.
That was about all we could take, and we just ran inside
To this very day, when I think about it, it sends shivers down my spine.
No wonder I had put it out of my mind for so long.
I'm sure I wouldn't have believed it, had I been on my own.
And others would have said I imagined it.
Thank goodness Mum saw exactly the same thing.
It just proved to me once again, that the "other side" was happening everywhere.
I guess it's just a case of whether your mind is open enough to see it, or you believe it enough to be true ....

There are many references to ghosts in Mesopotamian religions - the religions of Sumer, Babylon, Assyria, and other early states in Mesopotamia.
Traces of these beliefs survive in the later Abrahamic religions that came to dominate the region.
 The concept of ghosts may predate many belief systems. Ghosts were thought to be created at the time of death,

taking on the memory and personality of the dead person. They traveled to the netherworld, where they were assigned a position, and led an existence similar in some ways to that of the living.
Relatives of the dead were expected to make offerings of food and drink to the dead to ease their conditions. If they did not, the ghosts could inflict misfortune and illness on the living.
Traditional healing practices ascribed a variety of illnesses to the action of ghosts, while others were caused by gods or demons.

There was widespread belief in ghosts in ancient Egyptian culture.
The Hebrew Bible contains few references to ghosts, associating spiritism with forbidden occult activities.
Spiritism is a spiritualist and reincarnationist belief system that originated in France in the mid-19th century.
It is based on the idea that spirits exist separately from human bodies, and can be accessed through mediums. Spiritists believe that spirits undergo repeated reincarnation into the physical world, and that events in the material world are influenced by the spiritual world.

The soul and spirit were believed to exist after death, with the ability to assist or harm the living, and the possibility of a second death.
Over a period of more than 2,500 years, Egyptian beliefs about the nature of the afterlife evolved constantly. Many of these beliefs were recorded in hieroglyph inscriptions, papyrus scrolls and tomb paintings.
The Egyptian Book of the Dead compiles some of the beliefs from different periods of ancient Egyptian history.
In modern times, the fanciful concept of a mummy

coming back to life and wreaking vengeance when disturbed, has spawned a whole genre of horror stories and films.

The ancient Romans believed a ghost could be used to exact revenge on an enemy, by scratching a curse on a piece of lead or pottery and placing it into a grave.

Plutarch, in the 1st century AD, described the haunting of the baths at Chaeronea by the ghost of a murdered man.
The ghost's loud and frightful groans caused the people of the town to seal up the doors of the building.

Another celebrated account of a haunted house from the ancient classical world is given by Pliny the Younger (c. 50 AD).

Pliny describes the haunting of a house in Athens, which was bought by the Stoic philosopher Athenodorus, who lived about 100 years before Pliny. Knowing that the house was supposedly haunted, Athenodorus intentionally set up his writing desk in the room where the apparition was said to appear and sat there writing until late at night when he was disturbed by a ghost bound in chains.

He followed the ghost outside where it indicated a spot on the ground.

When Athenodorus later excavated the area, a shackled skeleton was unearthed. The haunting ceased when the skeleton was given a proper reburial.

In the New Testament, according to Luke 24:37-39, following his resurrection, Jesus was forced to persuade the Disciples that he was not a ghost (some versions of the Bible, use the term "spirit").

Similarly, Jesus' followers at first believed he was a ghost (spirit), when they saw him walking on water.

In the 5th century AD, the Christian priest Constantius of Lyon, recorded an instance of the recurring theme of the improperly buried dead who come back to haunt the living, and who can only cease their haunting when their bones have been discovered and properly reburied.

Ghosts reported in medieval Europe tended to fall into two categories: the souls of the dead, or demons. The souls of the dead returned for a specific purpose.

Demonic ghosts existed only to torment or tempt the living.
The living could tell them apart by demanding their purpose in the name of Jesus Christ.
The soul of a dead person would divulge its mission, while a demonic ghost would be banished at the sound of the Holy Name.

Most ghosts were souls assigned to Purgatory, condemned for a specific period to atone for their transgressions in life.
Their penance was generally related to their sin.
For example, the ghost of a man who had been abusive to his servants, was condemned to tear off and swallow bits of his own tongue.
The ghost of another man, who had neglected to leave his cloak to the poor, was condemned to wear the cloak, now "heavy as a church tower".
These ghosts appeared to the living, to ask for prayers to end their suffering. Other dead souls returned to urge the living to confess their sins before their own deaths.

Medieval European ghosts were more substantial than ghosts described in the Victorian age, and there are accounts of ghosts being wrestled with and physically restrained until a priest could arrive to hear its confession.
Some were less solid, and could move through walls.
Often they were described as paler and sadder versions of the person they had been while alive, and dressed in tattered gray rags.
The vast majority of reported sightings were male.

There were some reported cases of ghostly armies, fighting battles at night in the forest, or in the remains of an Iron Age hillfort, as at Wandlebury, near Cambridge, England.

Living knights were sometimes challenged to single combat by phantom knights, which vanished when defeated.

From the medieval period, an apparition of a ghost is recorded from 1211, at the time of the Albigensian Crusade.

Gervase of Tilbury, Marshal of Arles, wrote that the image of Guilhem, a boy recently murdered in the forest, appeared in his cousin's home in Beaucaire, near Avignon.

This series of "visits" lasted all of the summer.

Through his cousin, who spoke for him, the boy allegedly held conversations with anyone who wished, until the local priest requested to speak to the boy directly, leading to an extended disquisition on theology.

The boy narrated the trauma of death and the unhappiness of his fellow souls in Purgatory, and reported that God was most pleased with the ongoing Crusade against the Cathar heretics, launched three years earlier.

The time of the Albigensian Crusade in southern France was marked by intense and prolonged warfare, this constant bloodshed and dislocation of populations being the context for these reported visits by the murdered boy.

When I was 18 years old, in fact the day of turning 18, we finally moved out of that house.
I for one, could not wait.
Two of my brothers had already left to get married.
But they never forgot.

Our new home seemed so bright, fresh, and inviting, it felt really good.
But after busying ourselves putting the furniture in place, and making the house a home, the memories would start to surface again.
Wondering if the same souls that frequented and haunted the previous house, would follow us.
They didn't.
There were a few times over the next 12 years, where I was sure I had heard "things", or see "things" out of the corner of my eye.
But thankfully, it never amounted to anything terrifying.

For any of us.

But it didn't stop there ...

My brother Kenneth loved classic cars.
And his Mother-in-law had a garage that she didn't use, and said that he could keep it in there.
And so he did.
Where was this garage?
Yes, you've guessed it. At the top of the same street we had moved away from.

One Sunday afternoon, that was filled with bright sunshine, he decided to go and spend some time with his beloved classic.

He had been there a little while, when someone said hello to him.
He lifted his head out from under the bonnet, to see a long time friend (We'll call him Mark), walking over to him.
Kenneth asked him what he was doing round those parts, and he said he had just moved into the street.
"But there is something not right with that house" Mark said.
"Why"? said Kenneth inquisitively.
"It's bloody haunted, that's why" said Mark.
"Things move around the house on their own, noises all the time.
the kids say they see people in their bedroom, and I actually saw an old woman on the stairs one night, that frightened the life out of me".
Kenneth just stood there, shocked.
There were only certain people that knew of what we went through, in that awful house, but Mark wasn't one of them.
My brother looked at him, and quietly said
"I bet it's number 9 you live at" ...
"How the hell did you know that" !!! said Mark.

"Because that is the same house we lived in for years Mark, and the same things were going on".
Mark couldn't believe what he was hearing.
And they stood there a while, talking about it.

It makes me wonder just who is in that house.
Clearly, there were loved one's of ours, that had come back from the other side.
But there would be no reason for them to stay there, after we moved on, would there!
And so it seems that my Mum was right, when she said she felt there were ghosts in that house, that had no affiliation to us at all, only the building we lived in.
And clearly didn't want us there, and let everyone know this by staying there themselves, and scaring the pants off of everyone that seen, or heard them.
Whether they had lived there, or were from deep within the ground beneath, where we were told was once a very old cemetery, we will never know.

When I started writing this book, my whole plan was to go round and see the people that lived there (because they were friends), and actually get their accounts of everything, including one more look around for *old time's sake*.
When I told my Husband, my Mum, my Son, and my best friend my plan, every one of them begged me not to, and made me promise that I wouldn't go anywhere near the place.
Their fear was the fact that these lost souls just may remember me, and follow me home ...

After hearing them all say the same thing, and the fear factor of old, rising up with warnings to my brain, my plans changed accordingly, and I never went back.
My plan was to discuss things with them over social media, as they were open to this.
However, sadly a while later, Mark passed away.

Very young I might add.
So I haven't bothered the family since.

As I grew up, the feeling that my Auntie Louisa was by my side, never left me.
I felt her presence so strongly, sometimes it was very un-nerving to say the least.
So powerful, that at any moment, I felt like she was going to walk right into the room, for all to see.
It was always at it's strongest during night time.
Typical "ghost scenario" right?
When night time falls ...
But that was how it was.
The room would go very cold, and although I couldn't see her, I could feel her all around me.
It was almost like she was hugging me. Very tightly.
Sometimes, I felt like the breath was actually going to be squeezed out of me, like I was being smothered.
The strange thing was, although I was "full" of her throughout the day, I never dreamt about her, which was very odd.
Until I left home ...

I moved into my new flat, and although I was sad to leave my parents, I was so very excited at the prospect of having my own place.
When we had finished decorating, and the furnishings went in, it was perfect.
I loved it.
I had a flat warming party, where friends and family came to enjoy good music, good food, and a nose around the rooms.
Apart from the miserable man next door, that didn't

even like you having the tv on during the day, let alone at night, the three years I lived there, was lovely.

The last year I lived there, I found out I was pregnant with my Son, and I couldn't have been happier.
He was all I had ever wanted, to feel complete.
Family and friends were told I was having a baby, and we all celebrated together.
It was a very special time for me. And long waited for.
I knew however, that it would mean leaving my home, and finding a bigger one, as I only had one bedroom.
But now I had a baby on the way, I had to put him first.
So we just enjoyed the time we had left there, and looked into where we wanted to live when he was born.

It was during those final months, that I had a very disturbing dream...

I dreamt I was in the graveyard.
The local graveyard.
Where all my family that had passed on, were buried.
It was the middle of the night. Pitch black.
Just the moon sending rays of light down, that barely lit up the pathway ahead.
But as I walked through the small side gate, I started to feel very frightenend.
I couldn't hear a thing.
But I felt a raging anger all around me.
It was so powerful, that I felt like it went right through me.
I managed to take a few more steps forward, and then I stopped right where I was.
I couldn't move.
All the gravestones were smashed up.
Some graves had been dug up, and the coffins were sat by the gaping holes in the ground.
Some of them even had the lids open, and I could see

the bones of people that had been buried for a very long time.
I was absolutely mortified.
But I couldn't move.
The anger all around me grew.
And with it, came the strongest sensation that my Auntie Louise was the reason for all this anger.
The reason she had stepped into my dream, and shown me this awful vision.
She was SO ANGRY, she couldn't hold it in.
And she wanted to show me in detail, how it was making her feel.
I felt sick to my stomach.
I didn't know what to do.

And all of a sudden, at the point where I thought I couldn't take any more, I woke up.
It was morning.
The sun was shining through the bedroom window, and all was well with the world.
Except I was still drenched in fear.
My heart was racing, and I felt very sick.
It was like I had brought the dream back with me, and couldn't stop it.
It took a few hours for me to calm down, before I was back with the living. So to speak.
That had to be the worst dream I had ever had.
And I knew I wasn't going to forget it in a hurry.
I told my Hubby all about it, even though it didn't help to relive it so soon.
But I needed to share it with him. Because it frightened me so much.
He was very understanding, and tried to soothe me as much as he could.
But the fact that the whole nightmare seemed to be about my Auntie, he knew how much that would upset me.
She had had such an awful death, and so very young, that the thought of her being this unhappy in the next

life, was very concerning to me.
I tried to forget it, by keeping busy, popping out to the shops, and having a nice evening meal with Hubby

But that night, the very same thing happened again.
And the following night.
And the night after that.

By the fourth "dream", I KNEW, without a shadow of a doubt, that something was terribly wrong.
TERRIBLY WRONG.
I had never known anger like it.
Especially coming from *the other side*.
And for it to happen four nights in a row - That told me that my Auntie was trying to tell me something from beyond the grave.
I didn't know why, but suddenly, I felt that I had to go to my Auntie's grave. That very day.
It couldn't wait.
It was deeply upsetting, and somehow, I needed to try and find out why this was happening. Why I felt Auntie was so deeply angry and upset.
My Hubby totally understood.
And that afternoon, we went to the graveyard.

As soon as I got there, I felt something was wrong.
It was like my Auntie had a hold of my hand, and was pulling me faster, to get to her resting place quicker.
And then I saw why ....

The workmen had been up the cemetery, fixing fences, cutting hedges etc, but were nowhere to be seen.
They had gone home, but their tools were everywhere.
I got to the top of the hill, and rounded the hedge where my Auntie was laid to rest.
And there it was .....
Tools upon tools, bits of corrugated iron, shovels, forks, you name it, were all thrown across the ground -

Except most of them were all over the top of my Auntie's grave.
I was LIVID.
And clearly, so was she !!!
One by one, I picked them all up, and threw them in anger, up against the fence.
I couldn't believe they had done such a thing.
I tidied the grave up, put the flowers on that I brought for her, and I told my Auntie that I now understood why she had come to me, and needed my help.
I said "You can rest now Auntie Louise. It's all gone now.
Sleep peacefully darling. I love you"...

That night, I had a dream.
A different dream.
My Auntie came to me, thanked me, and told me she loved me.
Twice.
While holding me so close.
And the nightmare ceased ...
There have been other times, that my Auntie has come back to me since the nightmare.
But thankfully, better times! Happier times!
And I still felt her as strong as ever by my side.
Still watching over me since the day she left this world.

My Son decided it was time to be delivered.
I was about to become a Mother.
Although the pain was tremendous, and 24 hours of pure agony, he finally arrived.
My 7lb 1oz bouncing blue eyed blonde Son had us in tears, as he ventured into the world.
My Mum was desperate to be with me, but they would only let Hubby in.
So she waited patiently outside the room, with my Dad.
The moment they met their Grandson, the tears flowed again.

He was absolutely beautiful.
Not a wrinkle on his body, and perfectly formed.
I just knew he would be.
He was special.
He was mine.
Family and friends popped into the hospital throughout the day, with their gifts, cards, blue balloons full of helium, tears, and cuddles.
The best day of my life.
My beautiful Son had arrived.

By evening, I was exhausted.
My boy was in the little incubator next to my bed, sleeping soundly.
I couldn't take my eyes off him.
The most perfect being I had ever seen.
I needed him closer to me.
Being next to the bed wasn't good enough.
I needed him IN the bed !!
Where I could hold him.
When the nurses turned the lights down, and went off to check on all the ladies in the ward, I picked up my Son, and laid him on the bed.
I pushed the incubator right up to the bed, with a pillow in front of it, so there was no chance of him rolling out.
I put another pillow the other side of him, so I couldn't roll on him, and gave him his own safe area right next to me, and got back into bed next to him.
I knew from the moment I looked at him, he was going to be the reason I breathe for the rest of my life.
I laid there, all cosy, stroking his beautiful blonde hair, and gently touching his soft hands and face, while he slept soundly.
One of the nurses came by, and stopped when she see what I had done.
"Well look at you" she said to my Son.
"No doubt you're going to be the apple of Mummy's eye" ..

She smiled, called another nurse over, to see how I had him safe and close to me, and they let me keep him there.
I was in my element.
For a few hours at least.

I had to put him back into the incubator, before I went to sleep of course.
And I totally understood.
But I couldn't sleep.
This was the best day of my life!
I didn't want it to end.
So I just laid there, staring at him.

And then she came ...

I had felt her around me all day. So strong.
And there she was, in all her glory.
My beautiful Auntie Louise.
Stood by the incubator, looking down at my Son with so much love, and that special smile I had always remembered.
She loved us all so very much, when she was on earth.
And from beyond the grave, she was no different.
That love, and that bond was still there.
She took it with her, when she left us.
And it was the first time she actually showed herself to me.
She looked up, gave me the same loving smile that she had given my Son, and slowly disappeared, right in front of my eyes.
But not before I told her I loved her.

I was in tears.
But they were tears of joy.
My Auntie had come back, and given me the perfect ending to the most perfect day of my life ...

USUI SHIKI RYOHO ...
The Usui System of Natural Healing, known as REIKI, is a form of healing and spiritual awakening.

It was received and developed 100 years ago, by a Japanese man called Mikao Usui, and brought to the west via Hawaii in 1937.
It is passed on from one person to another, through specific initiation rites, teachings, and defined forms of practice.
The Japanese word *Reiki* can be translated as "universal or spiritually guided life force".
The Usui System, is a way of working with Reiki, for the healing of self, and others.

The word *healing*, is used in the sense of regaining harmony and wholeness.
Usui Shiki Ryoho addresses the whole person, physically, emotionally, mentally, and spiritually.

I am a Reiki Master, that has had the privilege of sharing some of this powerful and spiritual light that Dr Usui so thankfully passed down to us.

What does Reiki do?
Reiki helps to harmonise body, mind, and spirit, for yourself, or anyone you may want to help.

Reiki is a powerful and gentle healer.
Promotes natural self-healing
Balances the energies in the body
Balances the organs and glands
Strengthens the immune system
Treats symptoms and causes of illness
Relieves pain
Clears toxins
Adapts to the natural needs of the receiver
Enhances personal awareness
Relaxes and reduces stress

Promotes creativity
Releases blocked and suppressed feelings
Aids meditation and positive thinking
Heals holistically

How does one learn Reiki?
Anyone can learn Reiki !!
The word "learn" is not quite right, as most of us cannot just read about Reiki, and then be able to do it.

The ability to use Reiki is normally given via an "attunement" or "initiation".
When attending a Reiki course, the participant gets attuned/initiated, by a Reiki Master, through a simple process.
This opens him/her to receive and utilize more of the universal Life Energy.
The attunements have in themselves a very powerful balancing and healing effect.

Since energy spins at different levels, Reiki is normally split into 3 levels -

Reiki 1
Reiki 2
Master

Once attuned, your ability to use Reiki will never leave you!

Just a small introduction to something very important to my life.
My best friend introduced me to Reiki many years ago, and I have never looked back.
For me, on a spiritual level, it is wonderful, and opens my mind to many things that I didn't think I could reach.
One of those places, is a plain of relaxation I never

knew existed.

I would probably put it down to my childhood, growing up in the most unusual way to any of my friends, by being freaked out by the unknown, and the *other side* on a daily basis, and the reason why, then, and throughout the rest of my life, I had never really known what it was like to be calm. To relax. To be at peace with one's self.
Until I found Reiki.
In those quiet moments, when I feel I need to heal myself, I think my very soul dances, to a tune that never existed in me previously.
When Reiki takes me to the *light*, whilst healing myself, I feel like I am in a totally different world. A higher plain if you will.
The healing light is wonderful.
The warmth you feel within your body is so spiritual, in those moments, you feel at one with the whole universe.

When I feel anxious, stressed, or just not having a good day, for one reason or another, Reiki brings me such peace and tranquility.
I have been a terrible sleeper, for most of my life. Not surprising right !
However, at those times, where I am so tired I begin to feel really low, my body aches, my head hurts, and my eyes feel like they have popped out, and are seated on my cheek bones, and I cannot sleep, no matter what I do, Reiki is always the answer.
It releases the anxiety, and everything that is stressful, and instead fills you with waves of light that I can only describe as *Heavenly*.
It's like floating through space, without a care in the world, and a warmth that makes you feel like you are surrounded by a blanket of utter peace.

And then I sleep ...

But I have to say, for me, the most rewarding part of performing Reiki, is to be passing those wonderful experiences onto others.
To heal them. Or at least to try and heal them.
Some people can be healed without feeling a thing. Even when they don't believe whole heartedly, they have that surprised look on their faces, after the session, when they suddenly realise their pain or discomfort, has disappeared.

Others can become very emotional, and can react very differently after Reiki healing.
Some cry.
Some laugh.
Some fall into a very deep and relaxing sleep during the session.
And others can fall asleep quietly, but wake up crying for no apparent reason.
Everyone is different.
We are all unique in our own way.

You can lay your hands upon them.
Or you can keep them inches above their body, and yet many will still feel the warmth entering their very being.

Even *Distance Reiki* is performed, all over the world. The person needing the help, doesn't have to be in front of you.
You can have a picture of them. Know their problem.
And send the healing light across the miles.
I have known it to work very well.
My friend has healed family members this way.
I did it with my Father.
And i've done it with my Husband, when I knew he wasn't coping very well, and needed a little *boost*.
The first person to receive Reiki from me, was my Son, when he was a little boy.
He was up one night, with a very bad ear ache, and

couldn't stop crying.
He was so tired, but couldn't sleep because of the pain.
The medication hadn't worked at all.
And it was at this point, I decided I would see if I could help.

I laid him on his side, put my hands on his ear, and began Reiki Healing.
I could feel the heat coming down my left arm so strong, it even surprised me.
I closed my eyes, said my little ritual to myself, and asked Dr Usui to help me heal this soul.

It must have been 90 seconds later, no more than that, my Son stopped crying, and fell into a deep sleep.
I finished the healing session, and tucked him in bed.
I stayed with him through the night, and he never woke once.
And when morning came, the ear ache had disappeared, and my beautiful boy was 100% again.

From this moment on, I knew that I could help others.
And it felt SO GOOD ...
A few years ago, before the hideous lockdown we all had to endure, my friend was spending the day with me.
When she is with me, she is one of the few people in this world, that makes me feel *safe*.
Always has. Always will.

I was feeling a little under the weather that day, and she clearly noticed it.
So she decided to give me a session of Reiki healing, which was music to my ears.
I needed it so much.
I sat there, eyes closed, and immediately felt the heat on my body.
Coming and going in waves, from my head, down to my

toes.
It was GLORIOUS.
But, as I sat there, even though I couldn't see her, as I had my eyes shut throughout the session, half way through, I felt like my friend was on edge.
It was just a feeling that came over me, and I could sense it, even though we wasn't speaking.
The nervous cough.
The way her breathing seemed to be faster, and more urgent.
The way she moved around me a little faster, so that she could finish the session quicker than she had been up to that point.

I never said anything.
She finished the session, and although I was so relaxed, and didn't want it to end, I opened my eyes.

I could see something was wrong with my friend.
Her face was flushed, and she had a worried look on her face.

"Are you ok"? I asked her immediately.
"No, not really" came the reply.
I began to panic.
"What's wrong"?
Her reply shocked me to my soul ...

"Who is Louise"? She asked me, and just stared at me.
My eyes must have widened immensely, and suddenly, I was out of my state of tranquility, and back to reality.

"That was my Auntie that passed away" I quietly responded.
"Why"? I asked her.

"When I was half way through the Reiki session, I suddenly had the word LOUISE come from nowhere.

And then a second time, like it was said to me right up close to my ear. Like she was saying it to me" ...

I cried...

At that moment, I knew that my friend had completely opened up the inner me during that amazing Reiki session, and she suddenly felt my Auntie around her as much as I did.

I told her all about my Auntie. The terrible death that she had.
And how I had felt her with me all through my life, since she had passed.

We had a cry together.

This was something that I will never forget...
My wonderful friend is very psychic too, and has seen and heard many things in her life.
But her connection with my wonderful Auntie that day, even had her in pieces, as she felt the strength of a precious soul that had passed, that was still clinging to life.
My life ....

It didn't stop there...

One particular evening, I was sat in the conservatory, and was feeling very sorry for myself.
I hadn't had a good day at all.
It had been completely emotional, for one reason or another, and I had pretty much had enough.

Everything that could have gone wrong, went wrong.
I think I was experiencing every emotion you could have, all in one go.
Depression, anxiety, anger, everything but feeling happy.
And I couldn't shift it.
The day had got worse and worse, and I got to the point where I just didn't want to hear from anyone.
I felt like curling up into a ball, and sleeping for a year.
Be put into a time capsule, and let me sleep for the next 12 months, and when I awoke, I could be happy again.
It was THAT BAD.
I just couldn't control it, no matter what I did.
I won't go into detail, but it was one hell of a day.

Well, at some point, I must have actually been so exhausted, I fell asleep.
Which isn't like me at all.
Because around 2am, my Hubby woke me up, and asked me if I was ok.
I felt very drowsy, very worn out, and very confused.
I was trying to work out why I was asleep in the conservatory.
I didn't remember being in there.

And then I remembered ..
It all came flooding back.
However, I was feeling a lot calmer than I had a few hours before.
Which was rather strange in itself, as I hadn't been able to feel calm for the last 12 hours or so.
So I was at least glad for that.

But the way my Hubby was staring at me, began to worry me.
"What's wrong"? I said to him, getting up from the fetal position, stretching out my legs, and trying

to feel human again.

"Do you feel ok"? he repeated again, still with a look on his face that began to alarm me.
"Well I feel a lot better than I did earlier, that's for sure" I replied to him.
"But the look on your face is beginning to worry me. What's the matter, tell me"? I said to him.
But I really wasn't prepared for his reply...

"I came in to check on you a little while ago, and you were still sleeping.
So I sat over here and was just watching you.
Mandy, your Auntie was here tonight".
"My Auntie? Which Auntie? Why didn't you wake me up"?
"Because it was your Auntie Louise" ....

I couldn't believe what I was hearing.
I couldn't take it in.
What was he telling me!
My Auntie came to him?
I couldn't speak.
I just looked at him in shock.
My heart was racing, but I had to try and control myself

"What do you mean, she came to you?
While I was asleep"?
"No" came the reply.
"She came to you" ....

I thought I was dreaming.
"She came to me?
What do you mean, she was stood in here"?
"No" he said.
"She was inside you"...

My head was spinning.
I was trying to take this all in, and finding it very difficult, to say the least.

But I needed to understand what he was trying to tell me.
"How do you know she was inside of me"?
"You don't remember waking up, and talking to me"?
"No, not at all" I said to him, my mind was doing overtime at this point.
"So you're telling me that I woke up, without knowing about it, and had a conversation with you, while I was still asleep"?
"You opened your eyes, and looked up at me.
But it wasn't your face.
You spoke to me, but it wasn't your voice.
It was your Auntie Louise" ...

My Hubby seemed so shook up, I knew that he had been totally traumatised.
I didn't know what to say or do.
My legs had gone to jelly, and my mouth was so dry from panic.
I was in absolute shock from what he had just told me.

I won't go into detail about what my Auntie said to my Husband.
But one thing was for sure -
She had seen the state I was in, and had come to me.
Her spirit was so deep inside of me, I became her.
All my Husband saw, was my Auntie.
She had overtook my body, to the point of showing herself to him through my face, and my voice.
And it had rocked his very being.

My Hubby has had many experiences with the *other side* through the years, and is very psychic indeed.
I always said he got it from his Mum, God rest her soul, because she was exactly the same.
I could write another book, just on his experiences too.
But what he saw that night, in me, was the most powerful

he had ever experienced.
And believe me, he has stories to tell himself.

Seeing my Auntie in this way, frightened the life out of him.
He didn't know what was happening.
I guess at some point, he may have thought I was dead or dying, and my Auntie had come through to tell him.
I really don't know, because since that night, he doesn't like talking about it, or even thinking about it.

I tried to get him to tell my friend about it just the other day, and he wasn't having it.
He gets that look on his face, and goes very quiet.
My friend noticed this straight away, as she knows us so well, and didn't force the issue.
We moved on to talk about other things.

I'm still not sure of the full extent, to what happened that night, or what my auntie said to him.
I still feel there were things said that he hasn't told me.
But whatever the case, it clearly had an impact so deep, he doesn't want to re-live it ever again.

I have told those that are close to me over the years, how much I have felt my Auntie with me, and how strong her presence was.
But it is hard for anyone, to completely understand this, unless they have been through the same thing.
The energy around you, and inside you, is something you just cannot put into words, no matter how hard you try.
It is not of this world.

But one thing is for sure -
My Auntie loved me when she was on this earth.
And she loved me every bit as much after she left.

enough to stay with me all my life, looking over me, and clearly looking out for me.
And as frightening as that could sometimes be, as a child, and sometimes since becoming an adult, it makes me feel so loved.
It made me realise, without a shadow of a doubt, that when we leave this world, it is not the end.
For whatever reason, the spirit can come back.
It can show itself.
And it can still be full of the love it gave on earth.
Depending on whether it is a good spirit, or bad spirit of course, in which case, you get the Poltergeist's, that like to let you know they are around in other ways, that can frighten the living daylights out of you.
As I found out many times in that house I grew up in.

But to know that my Auntie had been with me all these years, and watched over me, is something very precious.
Her love is beyond anything on this earth.
And always has been.

Until now that is .....

When my Father passed away, I never realised life could hurt so much.
I felt like half of me had died with him.

My Dad loved life so very much.
He was the best Father I could have ever wished for.

When I was a little girl, I was absolutely petrified

of being sick.
Just the thought of it scared me, let alone it happening.
I always thought I was going to die.

But there wasn't one time, throughout my childhood, where he wasn't there, by my side, helping me through it.
Holding my hand. Speaking to me, soothing me, telling me everything was going to be ok.
"Just let it all out darling, and you will feel better".
He would hold me so tight ...
I truly don't know how I would have coped, had he not been there, when I was a little girl.
Mum was the very same. Couldn't stand being sick, or seeing anyone else being sick either.
Had she been able to face that, she would have become a Nurse, and she would have made the best Nurse you could possibly want or need.
She would have been perfect...
But you can believe it when I say, anything else, and Mum was there by our side too.
Even to the point of coming in with me, while I had an operation.

Yes, I'm biased.
But there isn't any parents in the world, that I believe could come close to my own.
I was born into love.
And for this I thank them to the day I die. And beyond ..

"I love you Mandy" ...

Those were the last words my Dad said to me.
Two days later, he was gone.
He fought till he couldn't fight no longer.
He died in his sleep, on a Friday morning, with my Brother by his side.
He was the backbone of our family.

He was everything.
And this world, and this life will never be the same without him.
He would help anyone.
He had so many loved one's and friends, they couldn't all fit in the church, the day of his funeral.

Dad grew up in the days of Al Jolson, the singer.
And from a very early age, when he had been to the pictures, to watch the great man on the big screen, he wanted to sing like him.
He was around 15 years old at the time.

He practiced and practiced whenever he could.
And you better believe me when I tell you that I have never heard ANYONE imitate Al Jolson as good as my Dad could.
He was amazing.
I have so many tapes of him singing, it would probably take me months so to play them all.
Precious.
Very precious.

In his later years, when I had grown up, and was singing and songwriting myself, I took Dad to a studio, and had him recorded, singing two of Al Jolson's songs.
He was so proud of them.
He had always sung acapella, or sang along while listening to Jolson.
So this was the very first time that he had been recorded himself, and with the music, without Jolson's voice.
He was MARVELLOUS
First time in a studio, and yet did both songs in one take.
The guys recording couldn't get over how good he was.
I was so very proud.
VERY PROUD.
He always wanted to sing to a big audience, but never

got the chance.
We gave him that chance at his funeral ...
I know he was there.
I could feel him.
Many people said they felt him that strong, that at any moment, it was like he was going to kick the lid off that wooden box, and burst into song.

So instead of hymns, we played our Father singing.
And when the songs finished, every single person in that church stood up, and was applauding through the tears.
Even the Priest.
The clapping rang all around the church, and seemed to go on forever.
Dad finally got the audience he wanted.
I just Pray he was there to see it.

The day he died, was like the world had ended, for me and my family.
I was at home on my own when I got the news that he had gone.
Family members were on the train, halfway here, that were coming to see him.
But it was too late.
When I was able to speak, I had to give them the devestating news that he had already gone.
So I arranged for them all to come to my house.
And I am so very glad that I did.
I don't think any of them will ever understand how much they helped me to get through that day.
All my Cousins were with me.
We played Dad singing all afternoon, and all of us had our own precious memories to speak of.
It was like our own special wake for him.
To honour him, and remember him.
The most awful day of my life, that I will never forget.
But helped along, with my hubby and my Son being there,

and my wonderful family that came to pay their respects to an Uncle they loved very much.

It was when they all left, that the realisation I was never going to see my Daddy again, hit me very hard.
The tears would not stop coming.
I felt so ill.
It must have been past midnight, when I went outside, just to get some air, because I felt like I was going to suffocate.
My nose was blocked. My head was hurting.
My eyes were sore. And my heart was broken into a thousand pieces.

I stood in the back garden, and sobbed again.
Only this time, I started speaking to my Dad, in the hope that he would hear me.
"Can you hear me Dad? Are you hear with me?
Remember what you always said to me.
That you would never leave me.
That you would always be here with me, no matter what.
I need to know you're here Daddy.
I need to feel you.
Tell me that you are here.
Tell me you have your arms around me right now.
Please Daddy, hear me" ...

It was pitch black in the garden, with just a touch of light coming from light down the side of the house.
I heard a noise, and looked around.
And in the one spot, where the light was shining, on top of the fence, sat the most beautiful Robin I had ever seen.
And the biggest.
I froze.
A Robin on my fence. After midnight. After asking my Dad to tell me that he was there with me.
I had my answer ....
That Robin sat there just staring at me, not making

a sound.
I cried again, and called out to my Dad.
"Thank you Daddy. I know that's you. Thank you.
I love you so much".

And with that, the Robin disappeared before my eyes,
and was gone...

A couple of days later, I was at home on my own.
Dad always said he would be watching over me when he
died, and to make him proud.
I was trying my best.

It was afternoon, and I was getting the clothes out
from the tumble dryer, when I just burst into tears.
It just wouldn't sink in that I wasn't going to see
him anymore.

And right now, I needed him.
I needed to feel his arms around me.
I couldn't stand it. I felt sick.
I slumped down on the floor, and was just looking at
the basket of clothes in front of me, that I had folded
up neatly, but just wanted to throw them all across
the kitchen.
Why .... Why did he have to die.

I called out to Dad, and told him I needed him.
I needed to feel him with me.
I couldn't stand it.
Still sat on the floor, I put my head down, and I
couldn't stop crying.

Then suddenly ... I felt like he was there with me,
holding me.
Instead of going cold, when spirits are around us,
I suddenly felt very warm, like he was all around me.
I lifted up my head.
And there in front of me, was a beautiful white feather.

It had come from nowhere.
And definitely wasn't there before.

Dad had shown once again, that he was with me, he was still around, and he answered me with his love.
And you know, for the rest of that day, I stopped crying, and felt Dad so close, it was almost like he was still here.

Still taking care of his little girl...

The day of my Father's funeral, my best friend wanted to be by my side.
Like she had always been, when I needed her the most.
I didn't think I was going to cope with the service, and break down.
I needed her strength so much.
I wasn't even intending on sitting at the front of the church.
Sounds absolute insane, I know.
But I have suffered with anxiety for many years, and when I'm stressed, it overtakes my life.
And when it hits hard, my eyes blur, my heart races, I feel sick and faint, and find it very hard to breathe.
All this was going through my head, as I was getting dressed that morning.

How the hell was I going to sit in a church, with my Daddy in a wooden box in front of me.

The anxiety was already on another level, and I was trying so hard not to be sick or pass out.
My legs were buckling, just thinking of the day ahead.

I had to make plans, to be able to cope.
I wanted my friend to sit at the back with me, in case I had to run out.
Planning - Always PLANNING.
It drives me CRAZY.
But this is how my life is.
And today, needed the biggest plan of all, or I was going to let my Dad down, and all my family.
I didn't know how I was going to cope with the worst day of my life.
I had to be strong for my Mum.
My Mum was heart broken.
My Brothers were in a state.
I needed to be strong.
We all needed to be strong.
"If they can do it, then so can I"... I kept telling myself.
But it wasn't working.
I was thinking ahead again.
And that's bad.
Wondering what in the world my family was going to say, if I didn't sit with them, and hid myself away at the back of the church.
They would never forgive me.
But I had to have a back up plan!
If I'm not strong enough to walk to the front of the church, then plan B would be my get out clause.
"At least I will be there" ... I kept telling myself.
I was in a mess.
I was crumbling.
I was absolutely petrified just thinking about it all morning.
But with no back up plan, I wouldn't have left the house.
My subconscious was in over-drive.
I just needed it to be over...

My friend was out of town that morning.

Always helping others, she had taken someone to hospital, but would have been back well in time for the funeral.
She had it all planned, and would be back way before the funeral.

Or so she thought, before the car broke down ...

We was all at Mum's waiting for them to bring Dad, and then go on to the church.
I felt a little better when I got to Mum's.
She is so so strong.
She makes me feel strong.
What she has endured in her life, not many people would have come out the other side.
And today, she was proving it again.
I could see the pain all over her face, as she was getting ready, with everyone in the other room.
She was struggling Bless her.
My God, it must have been so hard for her.
But she was holding herself together, and showing once again why I have wanted to be like her all my life.
I love her so much.

By the time we got to the church, we were all crying, even before we got out of the cars.
It was over whelming to see so many people, come to say goodbye to my Daddy.
He was so loved.

I was looking around for my friend.
I couldn't see her.
She wasn't there.
She hadn't made it.
Plan B had gone ...

I was left with no choice.
Now, I had to walk to the front of that church, when I couldn't even feel my legs.

My Mum said it was going to be ok.
I followed behind her, with my Son and Hubby.
Just seeing my Brothers carrying their Father made me sob.
How brave were they.
How strong were they being for their Dad.
I had to do the same.
"Give me your strength to do this Dad" I said to myself, and walked into the church, and up to the front, with the rest of my very brave, and very beautiful family, where I belonged.

Divine intervention again?

If plan B had been available, I probably would have taken it, and let everyone down.
If plan B had been available, I wouldn't have been at the side of my Son, when he broke down in the church, and needed me.
He was the apple of my Father's eyes.
There was no way that he was going to let me sit at the back!
Dad wasn't having any of it.
He wanted me right there, comforting his Grandson, and sitting with my Mum and my Brothers, where I belonged.
And he got his wish.

When my Son broke down, all my own negative thoughts disappeared.
He was doing so well.
But hearing his Grandad sing broke him.
It was all about him now.
I needed to comfort him.
Be there for him.
And thankfully, I was.
My strength returned.
Right when I needed it the most.
Dad would have been proud of me...

Later, me and my friend both agreed, that it was Dad that stopped my friend from being on time.
He knew me so well.
And was always one of the few people that understood my anxiety, and helped me so much.
But this is one day he needed me to be strong.
And once again, had a helping hand in it...

But it didn't help my friend.
She was mortified, by the time she got to the wake.
I had a job to control her.
She loved my Father so much.
And he loved her the same.
He would always say to her
"Look after my Mandy when I'm not here anymore"..
"I will always look after her" she would tell him.

So, although everything had turned out as it should, and I managed to stay strong, it wasn't helping my friend at all, bless her heart.
She just couldn't stop crying, saying she had let me down.
"No you haven't darling.
It was Dad's way of making me strong.
And you're here now"...

Me, Hubby, my Son, my friend, and a couple of other friends of ours, decided to leave the wake early, and go back up to the cemetery, to look at the flowers, and for my friend to say her own goodbyes to Dad.

The flowers were beautiful.
So many of them.
We read all the lovely messages from family and friends, and everyone except me and my friend went to sit on the bench nearby.

We stood at my Father's graveside together, and was talking to him.

My friend told him she was so sorry for not making it to the church, and couldn't stop crying.
I was trying to console her, but was having a job.

And then Daddy took over again ...

As I stood there, holding my distraught friend,
She suddenly said "Oh my God, I can feel your Dad's arm round my shoulder" ...
And at the exact same time, I felt, and said, the very same thing ....

It was AMAZING.

It was like he was stood behind us, his hands on both of our shoulders, holding us tightly, like he had always done in life.
He was reassuring us that he was still here.
Still looking after us.
Still loving us.
And most of all, to let my friend know, that everything was fine.

The tears kept coming.
But now for a different reason.

Daddy was there ....

I have one more very important thing to tell you.
The moment my Father passed over, my Auntie left me.
I haven't felt her since.
Not once.
She has gone.
And in her place, walks my Father now.
Beside me.

Like he always was.
Rest now Auntie.
I love you ... X

If I told you of all the events in my life, from the *other side*, it would be the longest book in the world! But I hope the parts I have shared with you, have helped you in the knowledge that when we leave this world, it is not the end.

We WILL see our loved one's again.
And they do still walk among us.

For some of you, this will help in so many ways.
For others, it may still be difficult to believe.

Open your mind. And have faith.
And that faith will be given to you, in all it's glory...

Love & Light

M.

CREDITS & ACKNOWLEDGEMENTS

East Coast Angels

Kira Cochrane

en.wikipedia.org

Pew Research Centre

Pixabay.com
The Reiki Association

Printed in Great Britain
by Amazon